Out of the Fog

**Fifty devotional thoughts on our freedom in
Christ from legalism and religion**

Recommendation:

Have you ever been in a dense fog? I can remember times when I thought I would never find my way out. Then, without warning, the fog begins to break; I could see patches of blue sky, and I could actually see my surroundings! It was wonderful.

That's how I felt after reading Scott's manuscript. It was refreshing. It was insightful. I saw patches of blue sky and my surroundings!

Chapter after chapter I discovered fresh biblical insights that revealed God's truth in man's context. The Scripture says, "Whom the Son sets free is free indeed." Scott gives glory to the Son in this book, and there is a certain liberating element contained in these pages — an element to set one free from the fog of perceptions and misperceptions of being a believer in Christ.

Christ is truth. Truth is simple and profound. It is cold steel; yet, at the same time, it is healing. "You shall know the truth and the truth shall set you free."

I believe that Christians bound in legalism who read this book will have an "ah hah" moment. I believe that Christians who read these pages and struggle with religion or church tradition will be released into new found freedoms. I believe that Christians who are living their life according to what is expected of them by other believers will be set free. Well-meaning individuals who have modeled and taught with true sincerity yet found themselves trapped in the periphery of following Christ without discovering the heart of relationship of following Him will now have a tool to help them get out of the fog and see their true surroundings. Through this writing I believe others will find a life of freedom and liberty in Christ.

I recommend this book to you not only because I have reviewed the chapters but because I know the author. His speech and lifestyle align themselves together. You will benefit from your reading of this book, and its value will not diminish because of worn out pages.

Greg Mundis, D.min.
Assemblies of God World Missions
Europe Regional Director

Acknowledgements
Editing: Eloise Neely and Mitch Stricker
Cover Design: Jason Nill
Inspiration and Censorship: Marisa Smith

I dedicate this book to my good friends and missionary colle•g•••Jacob Bock and Kevin Prevost who were a source of encouragement and who pushed me to do my best. And especially to Marisa, my wife of over 30 years, who believed in me and felt I had a message that needed to be heard. She returned all my half hearted attempts and my mediocre articles to me to be done right. I am a very fortunate man to have such good friends and such an excellent wife. Thank you Jesus for being so good to me.

ISBN: 978-0-578-01975-8

Out of the Fog

Fifty devotional thoughts on our freedom in Christ from legalism and religion

Scott Smith

Introduction

This book is written for sincere Christians, those Christians who longs to live a life pleasing to God. We have a desire to serve Jesus and express our gratitude for all He has done for us. However, many times pleasing Him feels like hard work and so we become tired or frustrated.

Hebrews 4:9 says that there remains a rest for the people of God. This rest is not for a spiritual elite, but for every Christian everywhere. Soaring on the wings of an eagle, running and not getting weary, walking and not fainting are not just goals, but are fundamentals necessary for the Christian walk.

Many times living the Christian life is reduced to prohibitions and obligations. The Apostle Paul had no patience for the people who defined the beautiful life in Christ this way. He was equally angry with those who abused grace to satisfy their carnal desires. Instead, the Christian life should be one that shines more and more until that perfect day comes. It is a life of being more than just a mere conqueror, but rather, an abundant life. To those of you who have felt that the Christian life is hard, that only those with a strong will can live it, there is good news. There is a new and a living way where His yoke is truly easy and His burden that He asks us to carry is truly light.

Read the first chapter. It will take you about three minutes. If you don't like the first chapter, you won't like the book. If you can identify with the first chapter, this book can help you, so read on! You will learn of the life of freedom and joy that walking with Christ can bring.

Scott K. Smith

scott.smith@agmd.org

Table of Contents

My Weariness Amazes Me (Bob Dylan)

My experience as a Christian has shown me that it gets easier every year to live the Christian life. On the other hand, trying to live the Christian life by your own effort gets harder every year. We get just a bit more weary every year.

This seems to be the experience of just about everyone who sincerely wants to be a good Christian, those who really want to please God, those who strive to live in holiness and make the Father happy. Those that don't have a sincere desire to live the Christian life to its fullest don't suffer from this problem of weariness. They have other problems, serious ones.

I was born again in 1970. I was 16 years old and for the first three years of my Christian life I did everything that I was taught: I went to church, read the Bible every day, prayed every day, fasted every week, witnessed to my friends... basically everything I was instructed to do to enhance my spiritual growth.

After three years I ran out of strength. I was very confused. What was I doing wrong? I was following everything that I was taught. I had been promised that I would have an abundant life[1] but what I really had was spiritual exhaustion.

I could only see two options. One option was to conclude that Christianity was not the truth. It was a legitimate option, but I had one huge problem; the Lord had healed me of several injuries that I had suffered when a train ran into my car. One evening, even before giving my life to Him, God healed me of a bruised kidney and bruised ribs that I had received in the accident with the train. I checked out the healing. I no longer urinated blood and I could breathe deeply without pain. God was real and He had healed me in a Christian church.

The other option was to conclude that I was not living the Christian life in the manner it should be lived. It seemed like my only option left, but I was confused. I had carried out everything that I had been taught in church and I had ended up without the strength to continue. What was going on with me?

One day as I read the Bible, I stumbled across a verse that helped me see my problem: "For it is God which works in you both to will and to do of his good pleasure."[2]

God produces the desire ("to will") and the ability to fulfill ("to do") that desire. But how?

I received further understanding from a verse I had memorized in Sunday school:

9

" I live; yet not I, but Christ lives in me: and the life which I now live in the flesh I live by the faith of the Son of God, who loved me, and gave himself for me."[3]

This life that I now live I live by faith in the Son of God. Or as another verse says, "faith which works by love."[4]

I had been "doing" the Christian life by my own efforts and, of course, I ended up exhausted. But, if I enter into the rest of God (Hebrews 3 & 4) "he that is entered into his rest, he also hath ceased from his own works, as God did from his."[5] The answer was to live by the faith "of" (not "in") the Son of God. Let Him carry me. That way I would have renewed strength, would mount up on wings of an eagle, would run and not get weary and would walk and not faint.

Now I still pray every day. I read the Bible every day. I fast every week, etc. The difference is that now He guides me in His paths of righteousness for His name's sake.[6]

---

1 John 10;10

2 Philippians 2:13

3 Galatians 2:20

4 Galatians 5:6

5 Hebrews 4:10

6 Psalms 23:3

10

Stunned by Grace

"I am really tired of waiting for my father to die." the son thought to himself. "I want my inheritance and I want it now." Sadly, his father gave in to his son's selfish plans and before the astonished eyes of everybody in the household, the son took off.

He had plenty of money for his trip so he went to a far land. He did not want to be watched nor helped by his family. He enjoyed to the fullest his new freedom and lived the life he had always dreamed of- parties, friends, sin... He delighted in the results of years of hard work by his father, wasting it all on a lifestyle totally opposite to that of his dad.

But wallking on the wild side expensive. The day came when he ran out of money. The parties ended and, just by coincidence, a famine struck the land. The son soon found himself without work, without food and of course, without friends.

He finally got a job feeding pigs. For a Jewish boy there was no more humiliating work. He even wanted to steal the pigs' food and eat it himself.

I love the phrase "he came to himself"[1] The kid finally got a clue and decided to look for work in his father's house. After a long, dusty walk, the son arrived back at home. When his father saw him, there was no chewing out or well-earned sermon. He didn't even allow his son to mention being a household servant. He just hugged his stinky kid, put the best robe on him, put a ring on his finger and shoes on his feet. The fatted cow was killed and the father organized a huge feast. The selfish, sinful, shameless son that had hurt his father so badly was received as if he were royalty.

Grace- very expensive for the father, free for the son.

Ready for another one?

Joseph's brothers hated him and caustically sold him into slavery to some nomads. Later, a series of circumstances landed him in the dungeon in Egypt. People didn't usually get out of dungeons in Egypt. Those were some pretty terrible conditions for a dreamer. However, when God changed his life and elevated Joseph, he told his brothers, "you thought evil against me; but God made it into good."[2] He knew that his brothers wanted to hurt him as much as humanly possible, but his faith in God led him to forgive them.

Grace- very expensive for Joseph, very good for his brothers.

11

Recently I was told about a man who had left God and was living in sin with his girlfriend. The guy was 28 years old. "How should we treat him?" I was asked. "Stun him with grace," I answered. "If he were 8 years old, you would have to 'train up the child in the way he should go'³- but at 28 it is different. You could try the world's tools so that he could "see what he has done", but that is NOT what God is doing. God is watching to see if he comes home. Jesus is interceding for him. With 'cords of love' He is bringing him back.⁴ Love him. Receive him. Let him know that there is nothing that he can do to make you love him less nor is there anything he can do to make you love him more. He has really hurt you, but forgiving 490 times⁵ is not a maximum, it is a minimum."

We are not authorized to use the weapons of the flesh- shame, intimidation and guilt. The Spirit convicts of sin, righteousness and judgement.⁶ Let's allow the Spirit do His work. Godly sorrow produces repentance.⁷ Let Him do His work without interference.

I have been wounded in the house of my friends many times. When a loved one, like the prodigal or like Joseph's brothers hurts us, it is hard to forgive and extend grace. Grace is always expensive... for the one who gives it. It is going to cost me, but I have to pay the price and allow others to go scot-free.

1- Luke 15:17

2- Genesis 50:20

3- Proverbs 22:6

4- Hosea 11:4

5- Romans 2:4

6- Matthew 18:22

7- John 16:8

8- 2 Corinthians 7:10

Joyful Joyful

I really believe that God wants us to know, on a deeply personal level, that He is a good God who loves us with all His heart, soul, mind and strength. He showed us this when He said: "For I know the thoughts that I think toward you....thoughts of peace, and not of evil, to give you a future and a hope."[1]

God created us with the ability to experience joy and happiness. His plan for His people has always been that we enjoy, we delight and we be happy in Him. Just as He did for David, He wants to change our mourning into dancing and gird us with gladness.[2] This dramatic transformation happens when we...

Read His Word: Jesus said, "These things I have spoken unto you, that my joy may remain in you, and that your joy may be full."[3] He wants us to find joyous fulfillment in His Word.

Fellowship with One Another: In the early days of the church, the believers found joy by "continuing daily with one accord in the temple, and breaking bread from house to house…with gladness and singleness of heart."[4] We can find joy in the same way.

Get Answers to Prayer: Jesus said "Ask, and you shall receive, that your joy may be full."[5] If you look, you will find that the phrase "that your joy may be full" is repeated many times in the Epistles.

Spend Time with Him: Yet another sure way to find joy. "You have made known to me the ways of life; you will make me full of gladness with your presence."[6]

The natural result of walking in the Spirit is joy.[7] "The kingdom of God is not meat and drink; but righteousness, and peace, and joy in the Holy Ghost."[8]

So, I have to ask myself, why are the people who emphasize holiness so cranky? These promoters of righteousness almost give righteousness a bad name. With fire in their eyes and one eyebrow raised (a talent that I have not mastered even after practicing for hours in the mirror), they stick their finger in your face and tell you with a thundering voice, "You must be holy as God is holy!"

Well, I want to be holy- but do I have to be bad-tempered too?

Jesus wasn't bad tempered. Hebrews says, "You have loved righteousness, and hated iniquity; therefore God, even your God, has anointed you with the oil of gladness above your companions."[9]

Jesus had more gladness than any of His companions! The Old Testament also talks about God being joyful: "The Lord your God in the midst of you is mighty; he will save, he will rejoice over you with joy; he will rest in his love, he will joy over you with singing."[10]

In one of the Psalms, it says, "But let the righteous be glad; let them rejoice before God: yea, let them exceedingly rejoice."[11] If I go a while, maybe a couple of days, without this joy and gladness, I worry. This means that my heart is getting hard. I need to go back into His presence where there is fullness of joy and pleasures forevermore.

And finally, at the end of my life I hope to hear, "Well done, good and faithful servant: you have been faithful over a few things, I will make you ruler over many things: enter thou into the joy of your lord."[12]

Let's serve God with gladness. Let's go before His presence with rejoicing.[13]

"Now the God of hope fill you with all joy and peace in believing, that you may abound in hope, through the power of the Holy Ghost."[14]

1- Jer. 29:11

2- Psalms 30:11

3- John 15:11; 1 John 1:4

4- Acts 2:46

5- John 16:24

6- Acts 2:28

7- Galatians 5:22

8- Romans 14:17

9- Hebrews 1:9

10- Zephaniah 3:17

11- Psalm 68:3

12- Matthew 25:21

13- Psalms 100:2

14- Romans 15:13

God's Rest

One of the errors that legalists commit is to think that we have to figure out God's will though Bible study and then strive to fulfill it.

In Philippians 2:13 I discovered a verse that opened my eyes to God's rest: "…it is God who is at work in you, both to will and to work for His good pleasure."

Until I saw that, I tried to produce in myself the desire (the "will") and then to dedicate all my strength to fulfilling it (the "work").

But that's not the way God wants it. He wants to create the desire to do His will in me, and then give me the strength to do it. Amazing! My job is simply to let the Potter's hands mold me however He wants.

When we allow God to work in us the will and the ability, it changes everything. It is hard for legalists to believe that "God is much better to me than I deserve." They might say it out loud, but they can't believe it in their hearts because it goes against their whole life philosophy. They truly believe that God is very good to them- but only when they deserve it. The blessings they receive come in exchange for faithfully serving Him, and not simply as unearned gifts.

A legalist believes that it is up to him to shape his life and ministry. These are usually sincere people and would say that God has made them what they are, but in their hearts they really believe that they are spiritually limited by their own level of sincerity and effort.

Remember in Luke 18:11, 12 when the Pharisee prayed? He told God that he was not a thief, that he was not unfair nor was he an adulterer. He fasted twice a week and tithed on all he received. Look again at that prayer. He started his prayer out giving thanks to God but at the end of the prayer, Jesus said that he was not "justified"!

As a friend of mine said, "We can be proud of our own works but we can never be proud of a gift received, just grateful."

God wants to work in us and through us. In John 6:29 we read that the work of God is to believe in Jesus. Paul emphasizes it by saying "For what does the Scripture say? 'Abraham believed God and it was credited to him as righteousness. Now to the one who works, his wage is not credited as a favor, but as what is due. But to the one who does not work, but believes in Him who justifies the ungodly, his faith is credited as righteousness,'[1] He goes even further

15

a few chapters later when he says, "But if it is by grace, it is no longer on the basis of works, otherwise grace is no longer grace."[2]

This work of grace does not make us lazy nor negligent, which is just what the legalists are afraid of. "And God is able to make all grace abound toward you; that you, always having all sufficiency in all things, may abound to every good work"[3] Works are a result of the abundant grace of God in our lives.

In Ephesians 2:10 we read, "we are his workmanship, created in Christ Jesus for good works, which God has ordained beforehand that we should walk in them." We don't decide what we should do, we walk in the works that God has ordained beforehand for us.

———————————————

1- Romans 4:3-5 (NAS)

2- Romans 11:6 (NAS)

3- 2 Corinthians 9:8

Fear

The most repeated commandment in the Bible is "Do not be afraid." However, in the last book — Revelation — the angel says, "Fear God, and give him glory."[1] And we know that the fear of the Lord is the beginning of wisdom. Obviously we are not talking about that fear which paralyzes us.

But there are fears in our lives other than the healthy and necessary fear of the Lord. It would be easy to believe that these fears are our friends, that they protect us, warn us and take care of us. But there is nothing further from the truth. They dress up as friends, but they lead us into slavery.

The feeling of fear can paralyze us. When we are afraid, the natural thing is to want to save ourselves whatever the cost. So fear drives us to make decisions that have nothing in common with the two great commandments in the Bible — loving God and loving our neighbor.[2] It incapacitates us to act out that selfless love. How many times in the Old Testament did God say, "Be not afraid of the words that you have heard"?[3] And how many times did the Israelites fail Him, submitting themselves to the enemy — because of fear — rather than believing Him or His prophet? Do a word search in your Bible program on "fear not". It is worth it.

There is a deeper danger that is less visible but still as deadly. God said in 2 Kings 17:35 "You shall not fear other gods, nor bow yourselves to them, nor serve them, nor sacrifice to them." We serve that which we fear. If we are afraid of getting sick, we might just end up constantly going to the doctor, taking lots of vitamins, imagining that every little pain has got to be the worst... We end up serving that which we fear.

If we are afraid of going broke, we try to earn as much as we can, to spend as little as we can, and we end up living like we are poor when actually, we have money in the bank. If we fear a certain person, our father for example, we will do whatever we need to in order to please him. If we see that pleasing him is impossible, we end up rebelling and cutting him out of our lives so we don't have to live without his approval. The same can be said for the fear of having no friends, the fear of boredom, or the fear of never getting married. We become capable of abandoning Christ in our hearts and going after these other "gods".

God wants us to trust Him even when the circumstances seem to be threatening. Jesus, when He was talking to His disciples about fear, always countered it by encouraging them to have faith, to trust.

17

The story is told of a certain animal trainer in London that acquired a boa constrictor for his act. He raised the boa since it was little and they became very close. One day, while on stage, as the people were applauding, a scream was heard and a crunching sound. The trainer's "friend", the boa constrictor had crushed him.

Fear is not a good counselor. The spirit of fear makes us doubt God. In other words our "good friend fear" crushes our faith and drives us to serve other gods, just like in the Old Testament. We serve that which we fear.

1- Revelation 14:7

2- Matthew 22:37; Mark 12:30; Luke 10;27

3- Isaiah 37:6

Total Access

Jesus said that the wind blows where it wants and even though we hear its sound, we don't know where it comes from nor where it goes. He then compared this to people that are led by the Spirit.[1] Have you ever heard a sermon on this verse? What is it trying to tell you? Nicodemus did not understand it and Jesus was talking directly to him.

In this 21st century, punctuality, five-year plans, Blackberrys (or Palm Pilots) are signs that you are a responsible person. To be able to tell where you will be next week and at what time you will be there makes you look important and in demand.

I am not against order. I have a daily routine when I am home and I do not stray from it one bit.

However, spontaneity is a very important part of being led by the Spirit.

There are some that like spontaneity because they are rebellious or have a hard time submitting to authority. They want to do whatever they please.

I, on the other hand, rebel against spontaneity because it interferes with my prayer time, my schedule, the work I have in the office, etc.

But the great men of God were unpredictable (another way of saying "led by the Spirit").

Jesus lived like that. He did nothing except what He had been shown by His Father.[2] (In the Greek, "nothing" in this verse means... "nothing"). He did not say anything except that which His Father had already said.[3] He was totally led by the Spirit. He did some things that were incomprehensible for the disciples and made the Pharisees crazy.

Jesus never used His "connections" (and boy did He have connections!) He lived submitted to the Father and led by the Spirit. He did not grasp being equal with God.[4]

We cannot aspire to being the only begotten son of God. But we can be led by the Spirit, and those that are led by the Spirit are the sons of God.[5]

So go ahead with your daily routine. Jesus had His daily routine. But open up to spontaneity. The Spirit can ask of you whatever He wants to. He is the Lord and we are the servants. The more you walk in the Spirit, the more evident it will be. You may just do some things that make no sense humanly speaking. Jesus left a huge revival in its rapid growth stage to go and minister to one man who lived in a cemetery.[6]

On another occasion, there was a great multitude listening to Him. He told them that unless they ate His flesh and drank His blood, they would not have life in themselves.[7] That grossed everyone out and so they went home.

These are inexplicable things for the human mind, but doesn't He say somewhere that His ways and thoughts are not like ours? They are so much higher than mine just like the heavens are higher than the earth.[8]

He knows better than I. So I am going to let Him lead; not my routine and not my agenda. I give Him free access to interrupt my life and plans whenever, wherever, and however He chooses. He is the Lord, I am the servant.

1- John 3:8

2- John 5:39

3- John 8:28

4- Philippians 2:6

5- Romans 8:14

6- Mark 4 & 5

7- John 6:53

8- Isaiah 55:8, 9

Waiting on God

Hey! Slow down! Put on the brakes! Sit down and take a deep breath. Don't run…there's no hurry. What's the big rush anyway? Don't the years fly by fast enough already?

Waiting is something that's hard for us to do. It isn't easy to listen to boring music on the phone while we are on hold, stand in line, or wait at a stop light until the guy in front finally realizes that the light has changed- five whole seconds ago!

Did you ever wonder what Noah did for more than a year in the ark- without TV?[1] The children of Israel didn't know how to wait for 40 days and 40 nights while the pastor was getting the word of the Lord so they put the associate pastor in his place.[2] King Saul waited seven days (SEVEN DAYS!) for Samuel and then got ahead of himself because the prophet was 'late'[3]. The Corinthians couldn't even wait for each other at the church pot luck.[4]

God does not panic. I cannot conceive of God pacing from one side heaven to the other, stressed out because He has so much to do on earth. Neither do we see Jesus in the Gospels running all over the place because He only had three years to fulfill His ministry.

It is not good to hurry. We often make mistakes when we hurry.

The Holy Spirit says, "make it your ambition to lead a quiet life and attend to your own business and work with your hands, just as we commanded you".[5] In another place, the Bible encourages us to "lead a tranquil and quiet life in all godliness and dignity. This is good and acceptable in the sight of God our Savior."[6]

When I allow the world to establish my pace, I cannot hear the voice of my Lord. I find myself not concentrating on Him, but on the ministry. There is no time for meditation. (The word 'meditation' is practically lost in our frantic society- but as a good friend once pointed out, most of us do it in a negative way…by worrying.)

God comes to your window in the morning. He comes leaping on the mountains and skipping on the hills.[7] He is excited to see you! So what does He want when he shows up so excited? Does He want to teach you something life-changing? Does he want to correct some of your faults? Does He want to give you important instructions for a special task?

Well, according to Song of Solomon chapter 2- No! He is not eager to do any of those things. According to that chapter, what He wants is for us to go out with Him and listen to birds and smell flowers. He is so in love with us that He just wants to be with us.

I'd like to be with Him too, but I'm a very busy person. I just don't have time for listening to birds and smelling flowers. I find myself thinking, "Lord, if you've got something important to tell me, then go ahead- but if not, You know I've got a lot of Your work to do."

I am sure there are days that He goes away like a sad and disappointed lover.[8] It seems strange, but I can actually break the heart of the King of Glory by refusing Him.

When that happens, all I can do is ask His forgiveness... and you know, He always forgives me. God has a lot of patience with me.

But I don't want to make it necessary for Him have to have quite so much patience w I want to be better than that. I want to be just as excited to be with Him as He is to be me. When He shows up at my window to see if I'm ready, I want to jump out of my bed, get dressed and go with Him.

How about you? When the voice of your Beloved calls tomorrow, will you let the worries of the world wait...while you go with Him?

1- Genesis chapters 7 & 8

2- Exodus 32

3- 1 Samuel 13:8-10

4- 1 Corinthians 11:21

5- 1 Thessalonians 4:11

6- 1 Timothy 2:2, 3

7- Song of Solomon 2:8

8- Song of Solomon chapter 5

The Principal Thing

Generally those who live by Biblical principles are extremely sincere in their desire to please God. But I have observed that living by principles, even Biblical principles can have two different results.

First, many times we depend so much on Biblical principles that we don't really learn to recognize the voice of God. This is not good because what God wants is for our lives and ministries to be based on knowing His voice and following Him.[1] It seems to me that it is much easier to be guided by principles than trying to know God and recognize His voice. We can substitute principles for knowing God and we make those principles the guides for our lives. Remember, however, that it is not those who are guided by principles but rather those that "are led by the Spirit of God" that are the children of God.[2]

Jesus Himself said that everything He did here on earth was in obedience to what He saw or heard from His Father and not something based on principles.[3] Jesus even broke established Old Testament principles by doing things like touching lepers[4] touching a corpse[5], or a woman who was bleeding profusely.[6] He also broke principles that were not written down like when He met with a woman all by Himself in the middle of nowhere.[7] (What kind of testimony was that?) And He did all this while being led by the Spirit.

We cannot substitute the most important thing in Christianity — the intimate, personal, daily relationship with the risen Christ — for recognized Biblical principles, and run our lives by them. Jesus died and ascended into heaven to open up a new and living way for us through the Holy Spirit. It was even better than the friendship He had with His disciples while He was in the world.

The other thing that I have observed is that apart from taking away the need to be led by the Spirit, that living by principles alone does not work.

Paul wrote that if you are dead with Christ from the rudiments of the world, why, as though living in the world, are you subject to ordinances, (touch not, taste no, handle no, which all are to perish with the using) after the commandments and doctrines of men? Those things have indeed a show of wisdom in will worship, and humility, and neglecting of the body, but (as the New American Standard says) "are of no value against fleshly indulgence."[8]

Many times we Christians use the word principles instead of "law". We would never say that we were living according to the law of God, but I have said and heard others say that we live according to God's principles (or as the above verse says, "ordinances"). So, it stands to reason that if we cannot be holy by fulfilling the law, neither can we be holy by following "principles". This sincere but legalistic way of living fails every time.

The answer to this error is in the verse previous to the one above, Colossians 2:19 which says, "holding fast to the Head" and being part of the body which is "supplied and held together" and "grows with a growth which is from God." How long has it been since you have waited on God for a personal word for your life? Are you living your Christian life by inertia? " The one who says he abides in Him ought himself to walk in the same manner as He walked."[9]

1- John 10:3-27

2- Romans 8:14

3- John 5:19, 19-22, 30, 36; 9:4; 14:10

4- Leviticus 13:45, 46; Luke 5:12, 13;

5- Leviticus 11:24; Matthew 9:25

6- Leviticus 15:19-28; Mark 5:25-34

7- John 4:7-27

8- Colossians 2:20-23

9- 1 John 2:6

The Principle Thing Part 2

In the New Testament we have an example of how principles can annul the will of God. Jesus was arguing with the Pharisees about the Sabbath, the day of rest. God wanted to bless His people with a day off. However, the Pharisees had created a series of obligations and prohibitions that stole all the joy out of having a day off every week. They had also given the impression that God is a demanding deity and is almost never satisfied with our efforts to please Him. The Sabbath, instead of being a blessing, a joy, a day off, became a rigid obligation that was ruled by a series of dictates that were almost impossible to fulfill. This created guilt instead of joy. Which of the agrarian peoples of those days enjoyed a day off every week? It was a day dedicated to God, but the emphasis became focused not on God, but on the rules.

Jesus broke the Sabbath rules by healing several sick people on that day.[1] He could have said to them, "Hey, let's meet tomorrow and I'll heal you then." His disciples also broke the rules by picking heads of grain on the Sabbath (that raised a protest from the Pharisees.)[2] In that incident, Jesus pronounced His famous quote, "The Sabbath was made for man, and not man for the Sabbath"[3] The principles of God were made for us; we were not made for the principles.

A modern day example might be that of going to church. A church service should be a joyful, happy event. But rather than hearing the attendees say things lik "I was glad when they said unto me, Let us go into the house of the LORD."[4] or "Better is one day in your house than a thousand elsewhere",[5] we hear pastors say, "You need to come to the church service", and that to those who are already sitting there in the church service!

The Sunday service is a fount of joy — God's people see each other, there is fellowship one with another, (something that is often impossible during the week), we get together to praise God as one, we pray one for another, we listen to the Word of God, there is then more prayer, more miracles...

However, when something is subtly converted into an obligation two things happen:

First, the obligation (the law) kills.[6] There are some very interesting verses like "the law entered, that the offense might abound." or as the New American Standard says, "The Law came in so that the transgression would increase."[7] What does THAT mean? Or what about the verse that says "the power of sin is the law."[8]

25

What should be a source of joy can produce impatience or crankiness. (We're going to be late for church!!!)

The second thing I have observed is if church attendance is rigorously obligatory, the quality of the church service will go down. A little kid asked his mother, "Mom, is the sermon over?" "Yes, dear," replied his mother, "but the preacher doesn't know it, yet."

I don't want a service that is to entertain the people with the fear that if they are not entertained, they won't return. I am not concerned about trying to please those people who need to be entertained in church. But I don't want a lame service, either. What sincere people want is true communion with the rest of their brothers, a time of worship in Spirit and truth, a time for effectual fervent prayer, the clear, concise preaching of the Word with conviction of the Holy Spirit, a powerful call to respond to what God has said — with conversions, if possible — and then even more fellowship with others. Every time I preach, my goal is that there never be a mediocre church service.

We have to encourage each other to know, and to "follow on to know the Lord".[9] Church attendance is a part of this following on to know the Lord. It is a means, not an end in itself.

1- Mark 3:1-6 (as well as many others)

2- Mark 2:23, 24

3- Mark 2:27

4- Psalms 122:1

5- Psalms 84:10

6- 2Corinthians 3:6

7- Romans 5:20

8- 1Corinthians 15:56

9- Hosea 6:3

Hierarchy

A number of years ago we showed a film strip outdoors near the church we started in Valladolid, Spain. It was one of those old timers that had a cassette tape with it. There would be a clicking noise on the cassette when you were to change the slide on the filmstrip. Even then, it was outdated technology.

But it was worth it. The filmstrip was made in France and we rented it from Campus Crusade. It was about a town in the Wild West. This town had a rigid hierarchy. Everybody had a button pin on them with a number. I don't remember if the mayor or the priest had the number one, but I do know that the town drunk had the last number. Everyone knew where they were in the established order and who was above them and who was behind them.

In the filmstrip, Jesus showed up in this town and they wanted to give Him a button with a number, but He refused. They offered Him better numbers all the time if He would just pin on the button. He refused their tempting offers over and over. In the end, they became furious with Him because He was not following the rules and so they killed him. The filmstrip ends by showing that many of the inhabitants of that town started unpinning their buttons having been impacted by the determination that they had seen in that Man who was willing to risk rejection, ostracism and even death to remain faithful to his decision.

One of the "advantages" that legalism offers is that it allows you to know just who is above you and who is inferior to you. Legalism creates a hierarchy, it creates order.

Jesus refused to participate in this. He does not insist on His place in the pecking order. He is a servant.

When the final night came that He was to be with His disciples, He took the lowest place among all of them and showed what was in His heart. He did the worst job — maybe it can be compared to cleaning the toilets in the church building — which was washing the others' feet. That was a slave's job, and not just any slave, but the slave that had the least favor in the household. John tells us how He rose after supper, laid aside His garments and took a towel to gird Himself. He then began to wash the disciples' feet and to wipe them with the towel He was using to cover Himself.[1] This was extremely awkward for the disciples and they didn't know what to do.

If Jesus did that, who in the world am I, even though I am an ordained minister of the Gospel, to refuse to do any job in the church? How on earth can I think that certain tasks are for the newcomers or for the people in the church that have an inferior number on the button pinned on them?

What does it mean when it says that we should with humility of mind regard one another as more important than ourselves?[2] How far do we go with this? I am a minister, but I do not see my position in the Body as superior to that of anyone else. I just have a different job to do. Some are eyes, others are ears...[3]

Even Apostles, Paul was one of them, did not consider themselves as superior to anyone. Paul wrote saying that he felt that God exhibited the apostles as the last of all, as men who were condemned to death, as a spectacle to the world.[4] He also referred to himself and the rest of the apostles as the scum of the earth, the dregs.[5]

The disciples fought to obtain a higher place in the hierarchy.[6] They strived to obtain a place in this world and in the world to come.[7]

God help us to not do the same as the disciples! God help us to unpin the button when we gather together, gird ourselves with the towel, and serve the least of our brothers.

1- John 13:4, 5

2- Philippians 2:3

3- 1 Corinthians 12:14-26

4- 1 Corinthians 4:9

5- 1 Corinthians 4:13

6- Mark 9:34; Luke 9:46

7- Matthew 20:21; Mark 10:37

Practical Holiness

C. S. Lewis said in his book, Mere Christianity, "No man knows how bad he is till he has tried very hard to be good. You find out the strength of a wind by walkin against it, not by lying down."

Often Christians who sincerely want to please God make the big mistake of believing we can overcome weaknesses just by identifying them, analyzing them, and eliminating them little by little from our lives.

It doesn't work. It has never worked. It will never work.

If a person is fearful, as much as they apply themselves, will they quit being afraid? If a person is resentful or bitter, even if they identify the problem, analyze it, read books about it and get up every morning determined to not be bitter all day long, will they be able to avoid it? I am afraid not. We can say the same for someone who is worried about their health or someone who has a very bad temper, just to mention another couple of examples. For all our determination, for all our efforts, we will not be able to eliminate these carnal aspects of our lives.

A mother who gets up one morning and decides that she is not going to be angry with her children all day will undoubtedly find sufficient motives to get her really upset, maybe even before breakfast. A man who decides not to have an impure thought all day will surely find that he doesn't last even until lunchtime.

What are we to do, then? Should we just give in to sin?[1] Should we continue to struggle futilely thinking that this is what it means to be a Christian and that someday we will be able to enjoy a new nature that doesn't suffer from these endemic tendencies of human nature? We can cry with Paul, "O wretched man that I am! Who shall deliver me from the body of this death?"[2]

There is an answer and it is in the eighth chapter of Romans. It says that the law of the Spirit of life sets us free from the law of sin and death. See, what the Law couldn't do because the flesh is weak, God did for us. He sent His Son with the same tendencies we have and made Him an offering for sin. He conquered sin in the flesh so we can fulfill what the Law requires of us as long as we walk in the Spirit and not in the flesh.[3]

Let me give you an illustration. There was a man who had a black dog in his house. One day the man brought home a white dove and from that very day the black dog and the white dove fought constantly. Some days the white dove won the fight and some days the black dog won. His neighbor after seeing this constant fighting going on asked the man, "How is it that some days the dove wins and some days the dog wins? What makes the difference?" The man answered, "It depends on who I feed the most."

If we walk in the Spirit, the Spirit wins and we are free from the law of sin and death.[4] Free! Envy, gossip, bad temper, bad thoughts, worry, etc. are defeated, not by eliminating them through our will power but because the White Dove, the Holy Spirit, defeats them and throws them out.

This "more than conquerors"[5] thing is not utopian. The abundant life[6] is not only for when we are in heaven. Overcoming sin is impossible for me because my flesh is weak.[7] God has condemned sin in the flesh so that righteousness can be complete in us.[8]

Jesus not only eliminated sin, He also eliminated the power of sin in our lives.

Feed the dove!

1- Romans 6:1

2- Romans 7:24

3- Romans 8:1-4

4- Romans 8:2

5- Romans 8:23

6- John 10:10

7- Matthew 26:41

8- Romans 8:3,4

Liberty or License?

All of us believe that God loves us unconditionally. However, when we speak words like "Nothing you could do would make God love you less." it suddenly is not just an abstract idea, it becomes a risky truth.

License is a dangerous possibility under grace. The Epistles are just as hard on people who abuse the liberty God has given us as an occasion for the flesh as they are on the legalists.

Legalism does not work. It enslaves. But the law of liberty can be very risky.

We have the same goals as the legalists do. We want to please God. We desire to be holy. We want to be useful to Him. But we go about it in a different way.

I have a good friend — someone I admire for her commitment to God and her life of worship. She asked me a while ago, "What difference is there between legalism and holiness?" My answer was that both are after holiness in our lives, but the way we go about obtaining it is different. Are we going to be holy by striving or by resting?

We have to defend our liberty. We are no longer under the law of sin and death.[1] We are now under the law of liberty.[2] Paul warns us that there are those who come in to spy on the liberty that we have in Christ and to take us back into slavery under the law.[3]

They do not understand our freedom and they assume that what we are looking for is to be able to sin, to live a loose, carnal life.

We have to stand fast in our liberty wherein Christ made us free and not be subjected again to the yoke of bondage.[4] There are real and present dangers that threaten our walk in the Spirit.

There are some who would judge you for not submitting to rules like "don't touch that, don't eat that, don't handle that."[5] These rules look like they are good for denying ourselves, being humble and subjecting the flesh, but are of no value at all in overcoming carnal tendencies.[7]

There is a lot in the New Testament that deal with these two ugly substitutes for the real Christian life — legalism and license. The true law of liberty is where we need to walk.

So, let us stand fast in that liberty with which Christ made us free.[4] How do we do that? Again, the answer is by walking in the Spirit. We have to be sensitive to Him. We need to live the life in the Spirit.

God is Spirit and wherever the Spirit is there is freedom.[8]

1- Romans 8:2

2- James 1:25

3- Galatians2:4

4- Galatians 5:1

5- Colossians 2:22

6- Colossians 2:23

7- James 1:25

8- 2 Corinthians 3:17

The Snare of Pride

For me, the scariest sin is pride. It scares me because it is so deceitful. When I sin in other ways — for example when I am unfair to Marisa — I feel bad. But when I fall into pride, I feel great!

Someone once said that pride is the only disease that makes everyone else sick except the one who has it. Everyone can tell when I get proud. And it seems like they all have the "ministry" of putting me in my place, too. Have you ever walked down the street and seen someone with an attitude that said, "I'm the best thing going"? You probably felt like asking him, "Just who do you think you are?" Yeah, you wanted to put him in his place.

Well, there is a verse that speaks to such an attitude and it terrifies me. It says that God resists the proud but gives grace to the humble.[1] It is not only people who resist the proud, but God does, too. God is committed to resist me when I am proud. That is awful. The only hope I have to ever be a good person is God and He resists me.

I can see I am getting into a prideful attitude when all of a sudden everything irritates me. I start thinking that I deserve better. It seems like others are not treating me the way they should. Don't they know who I think I am?

Normally this bad disposition is not just seen by getting mad — although the wrath of man does not ever bring about the will of God.[2] I begin to manipulate. I want my own way. I want to intimidate and scare so that others do what I want.

What do I do to fight against this sin of pride? (I believe that pride is my greatest enemy.)

1) Be grateful. I need to express my thanks out loud. Pride is never grateful. When I see that someone has done something thoughtful for me, I want to and need to recognize it and express gratitude.

2) Ask forgiveness. Pride never wants to ask forgiveness. So, I say I am sorry for insignificant things (as seen from my perspective) such as being unfair to Marisa. It always feels good to the other person when I ask forgiveness and for some reason, what I have done that was insensitive never seems insignificant from their perspective. My flesh resists this ferociously, but asking forgiveness always reminds me that I am not nearly as important as I sometimes think.

3) Praise God. I cannot praise God with thanksgiving and continue in arrogance.

33

If I sit in my chair, turn off the light, wind down and begin to praise Him for my salvation and all of the blessings He has brought to my life — the greatest blessing from Him is Marisa — I can observe changes in my attitude. He is good. He is just. He is merciful and I recognize this and that puts me in my place, just where I need to be.

4) Praise others. I say, "You sure do a good job" to the waiter (when it is true), or "You are funny" to those who are, or "You know, I never thought of that". It has to be true, but these observations do come to my mind. I just make myself say them out loud. It is good for me to say these things and it is good for the other person to hear them.

Jesus said that whoever falls on the stone will be broken but whoever the stone falls on will be crushed.[3] God loves us. If we do not fall on the stone ourselves, He loves us enough to do whatever needs to be done so that we do not continue on in the sin of pride. If we do continue in pride, He will resist us and that is not His desire.

1- James 4:6

2- James 1:20

3- Matthew 21:44

34

What's in it for me?

Of course, the central point of Christianity is Jesus and not me. I am saying that "of course" to myself here.

My heart is deceitful above all things and to top it off, desperately wicked.[1] That verse in Jeremiah continues with the question, "Who can know it?"[1] My heart deceives not only others, but even me. Constantly.

The most dangerous and subtle deception starts when I substitute the desire to know and love Jesus more than anything else for the practicality of what He can do for me, what I can get out of this. Even though God has made us many incredible promises — and I like them all — it should not be the promises that I am after.

Let me try and explain myself. Jesus gives me peace. Honestly, I have become used to having peace inside. So, when I am not at peace, I seek the Prince of Peace — the one who is my peace — to get it. But in that moment, my motives for seeking Him have ceased to be unselfish. I am after peace. Jesus becomes the means to obtain that peace that I am accustomed to having in my life.

Another example is that when I have to minister, I need the anointing (if I am not anointed, it is going to be a long, dry sermon.) So, I seek Jesus, but not for who He is, but to get the anointing. Also, He is an excellent guidance counselor. However, seeking God's will can take the first place in my life that should be occupied by knowing Him and loving Him. In my case, it happens.

This is kind of like someone who marries a rich person for their money. They are not in love with the person, but in love with what that person can give them.

This must hurt Jesus.

Many times I see myself in the Gospels. I identify myself with the apostles when they were after all the benefits of being His. Jesus had to rebuke them, at times harshly.

Unselfish love is out of my reach.

So I ask for help, every day. I get up early and dedicate time every day to being with Him. I don't do this because I am spiritual, I do this because I am carnal. I need the Spirit to correct me. There is no hope for me if God Himself does not direct my heart into the love for Him and the patient waiting for Jesus.[2] I need

35

Him to do a miracle in my life every single day to be able to fulfill the first and second commandments. I have the tendency to read His Word looking for material for my ministry when the purpose of the commandment is to love God out of a pure heart, a good conscience and genuine faith.[3] I need love, a good conscience and genuine faith. Desperately.

It is tough. Jesus has made us so many promises and they are so good. All of them. But it is much better to dedicate my life to knowing Him as this, on top of it all, brings all the good things with it — peace, anointing, knowledge of His will and many, many other things. God, please guide my heart to your love.[2]

"It's not because of who I am but because of what You've done. It's not because of what I've done but because of Who You are." (Casting Crowns)

1- Jeremiah 17:9

2- 2Thessalonians 3:5

3- 1Timothy 1:5

36

Don't Move Until You See It

I have dedicated myself to being sensitive and obedient to the Spirit for years now. I want to be led by the Spirit in the sermons I preach, in what I say to people when I am witnessing and generally, in everything I do. One of the foundational scriptures for my life and ministry says that they who are led by the Spirit, they are the children of God.[1]

A good friend of mine helps me by sending out birthday cards to the preachers' kids here in Spain. We started a preachers' kids' association several years ago. She is a preacher's kid and the mother of preacher's kids. She told me that she tries to be sensitive to the Spirit so that every card that she sends out to the different children of the ministers here in Spain has a specific prophetic word for that kid. Every card, without exception.

Kevin Prevost, one of my best friends, made me watch a DVD several years ago of a movie entitled "In Search of Bobby Fisher". In those years, the U.S. was looking for a chess prodigy to compete with the Russians who were the world chess champions.

They found a boy, about 10 years old, playing speed chess in Central Park in New York City. Speed chess and tournament chess are almost two different games. They are incompatible. So they gave this prodigy a coach to teach him how to compete in tournaments and to get rid of the bad habits he had picked up playing in Central Park.

It worked. At the age of 12, the boy got to the finals of the national championships for his age group. For the first time, he was going to play chess in front of TV cameras. He was nervous.

The coach gave him some advice, very valuable advice, not only for playing chess. This same advice can be applied to those of us who desire to walk in the Spirit. The coach told the boy, "Don't move until you see it."

I have applied this wisdom to my life. I might feel pressured to just do something…anything. I might be feeling the heat of the bright lights. But if you move a pawn without seeing where you want to go, you can wreck everything. Don't just do something...stand.[2]

There have been times in my life when I was doing something "good", then I would suddenly realize that God had something else in mind for that moment. I couldn't do His will because I was already committed to what I was doing. Very

37

sad. Like the old saying affirms, "The good is the enemy of the best."

So I wait on God and I wait for God. Like the eyes of the servants look to their master to see what he wants, my eyes look to You, oh God, until you are gracious to me.[3]

This is the only way I know to avoid the trap of legalism; we need to know what He wants, when He wants it, and how He wants it done. He knows what He is doing. He has years of experience. I trust Him implicitly.

1- Romans 8:14

2- Ephesians 6:13

3- Psalms 123:2

Risen with Christ

Two friends of mine who have earned their degrees in Hebrew, tell me that the words we choose when we speak affect our thought process. I am afraid they are right. A good example of this is when we call the building we congregate in "the church". This affects the way we see that place.

Many times we hear "Jesus is my faithful friend" which is an amazing truth. But then we hear things like, "When I am weary, He gives me strength. When I am troubled, He gives me peace. When I am afraid, He covers me, etc."

These sayings, verbalized so often, are basically saying that Jesus gives me what I need when I need it. This is true, but I think that we need to go much deeper in the way we see things.

Jesus not only gives me peace, He is my peace.[1] He not only helps me, He is my help.[2] He is my song[3], my refuge[4], my praise[5]. He does not only show me the way, He is the way[6]. He doesn't just reveal His truth to me, He is the truth[6]. He doesn't just give me life, He is my life[6] and my salvation.[7]

This is much more than just a question of semantics. Either Jesus is with me in my struggle to do His will, or He is doing His will in and through me. In Hebrews 13:21 it tells us that He equips us in everything good to do His will and that He works in us that which is pleasing in His sight. He is either at my side, encouraging me, giving me strength, protecting me, or He is my strength[8], He is my fortress[9], my rock[10], my shield.[9]

Jesus wants to be all in all for me and if we reduce Him to just being a provider, it could happen that we only go to Him when we need something.

Henry Blackaby, in his excellent book "Experiencing God" emphasizes the verse in John 17:3. "This is eternal life, that they may know You, the only true God, and Jesus Christ whom You have sent." (KJV)

It all depends on Him. He guides me in paths of righteousness for His name's sake. If I allow Him to do it, He makes me righteous. My own efforts to be righteous have failed spectacularly. He has given us everything. He has provided everything.

Do you feel a burden for the lost? He tells us that if we follow Him, He will make us fishers of men.[11] So, can we say that if we are not fishers of men, that means that we are not following Him? I think we can.

Are you tired of trying to live the life that He expects from you? Has that struggle led to spiritual weariness? I have good news for you. There is a solution. He told us that if we go to Him, if we are weary and heavy laden, He will give us rest.[12]

Let's go to Him and allow Him to give us that rest.

1- Ephesians 2:14

2- Psalms 63:7

3- Psalms 118:14

4- Psalms 62:7

5- Jeremiah 17:14

6- John 14:6

7- Psalms 27:1

8- Psalms 27:1

9- Psalms 28:7

10- Psalms 22:2

11- Matthew 4:19; Mark 1:17

12- Matthew 11:28

Best Friends Forever (BFF)

Ever since the beginning, God had a close friendship with Adam. The Lord really enjoyed this communion with him during the daily walks they enjoyed in the garden.

This friendship with man is something that God likes a lot. But... the saddest day in history arrived and God lost His intimacy with His friend — Adam chose Eve over God — a friend who was made in His image. "Adam, where are you?"[1] This question, even though it is rhetorical, is a deeply sad one. God was looking for His friend.

In Proverbs 18:24 it says that a man who has friends has to show himself friendly. Jesus is very friendly. We can see this all over the Gospels — children feel comfortable with Him[2], He was "accused" of being friends with traitors and sinners[3], and the same night that Judas betrayed Him, Jesus called him "friend".[4]

I want to be a servant of God. I want to know His will and to seek to be more like Him. But all of this is just a part of a larger goal; I want to be a friend of God.

However, if I want to be His friend — and this is what I want the most in the whole world — I have to show myself friendly. To do that I have to spend time with Him, not to fulfill an obligation or a commitment, but to develop this friendship. I have to listen to Him speak through His Spirit and His Word. Friends listen to each other, they share their lives with each other.

So I am going to take care of and cultivate this friendship and make sure that nothing muddies it up. This means that I will have to quit being friends with the world.[5] And you know, it is not that big of a sacrifice because my Friend deserves that and more. As I become more and more a friend of God, the world loses its allure.

I voluntarily lay my life down for my friend. This gets easier and easier to do because my friend tells me "Fear not; I will help you."[6] He also says, "Greater love has no man than this, that a man lay down his life for his friends."[7]

Another thing that makes everything much easier now that I am a friend of God is repentance. I offend God much too often and, personally, it is easier for me to ask forgiveness of a friend that I want to please than to ask it of an indignant deity. It is also easier to receive forgiveness from a friend and really feel forgiven.

41

A great verse is John 15:15, "Henceforth I call you not servants; for the servant does not know what his lord does: but I have called you friends; for all things that I have heard of my Father I have made known unto you." I am not interested in merely following His advice, I want to know what my Friend is doing and do it with Him!

I gave my life to the Lord 38 years ago and what I really want is more clear to me now than ever. I have followed Him and I have served Him, but now what I really want is to be His friend.

Proverbs 17:17 says that a friend loves at all times. God loves me at all times and I, because I am His friend, want to do the same for Him. The transition from servant to friend changes everything. A servant obeys orders. A friend wants to please the friend whom he loves.

He is my friend and I really love Him.

1- Genesis 3:9

2- Mark 10:14

3- Matthew 11:19

4- Matthew 26:50

5- James 4:4

6- Isaiah 41:13

7- John 15:13

Paul's Dilemma

In Acts 15, the Apostle Paul is found in a moment of decision. Where should he go next to preach the Gospel? Paul had to deal with two powerful influences in making this decision: 1) What will people say? and 2) What about biblical principles? These are two influences we usually consider when we have a choice to make, but we see that Paul rejected them both and made a right decision.

In those days, Paul had taken on two new companions in ministry — Silas and Timothy. This was to be their first missionary trip together. Paul proclaimed, "We are going to preach the word in Asia." However, the Spirit contradicted him and forbade him "to preach the word in Asia"[1] What would his new associates think if he told them that they weren't going to Asia after all?

Paul paid no attention to their possible opinions of him but he obeyed what the Spirit commanded. Later he had a dream that showed him that they were to go to Macedonia.[2] If he had wanted to maintain his image, he didn't have to mention anything about a dream that only he had seen.

Wanting to look good or the fear of what others might say are a terrible basis for making a decision. The Scriptures specifically prohibit us from doing this. Public opinion should not be the reason for anything we do. Jesus rebuked those that did this saying, "How can you believe, when you receive glory from one another and you do not seek the glory that is from God?"[3]

If Paul had given in to the natural desire to look good in the eyes of his new ministry associates, he would have totally missed the will of God. Worrying about what others say enslaves us to a master that is never satisfied.

Another option that Paul had in order to look good in his brothers' eyes was to grab ahold of a biblical principle. Jesus did teach that the believers were to "make disciples of all the nations", didn't He? Wasn't Asia part of those "all nations"? Wouldn't going to Asia be in obedience to Biblical principles? But instead, Paul allowed the Holy Spirit to interpret the command and spiritual principle by sending him specifically to Macedonia and not to Asia as he had previously announced to his teammates.

In every decision I make, I face these two temptations — to please people by doing what they expect of me, and to make my decision based exclusively on biblical principles (and I know them well) without consulting with the Sprit (leaving Him without the option of interpreting and guiding as He wills.) To base my decisions exclusively on principles and precepts is much easier and requires less effort on my part. It is easier for others to understand and accept my decisions. Things get complicated when we talk about the importance of being led by the Spirit, especially when we have to correct something that we had previously announced.

Walking in the Spirit not only frees us from the slavery of pubic opinion and the legalism of principle, but it also just plain works. The person who walks in the Spirit can say, without arrogance or rebellion, "We must obey God rather than men."[5] We can also declare "In God have I put my trust: I will not be afraid of what man can do unto me."

Only God can give me the courage to ignore public opinion, politics, and precepts and the faith and strength to listen and obey the still, small voice of the Spirit.

1- Acts 16:6

2- Acts 16:9

3- John 5:44

4- Matthew 28:19

5- Acts 5:29

6- Psalms 56:11

Its All About You, Jesus

The Pharisees received a strong rebuke because they loved the praise that comes from men more than the praise that comes from God.[1] One Pharisee prayed, thanking God that he wasn't like other men, especially like the sinner standing next to him who was praying a prayer of repentance.[2] I can be even worse than that. I have thanked God that I am not like that Pharisee!

Right now I have to be careful. Two friends and I are starting up a new ministry. I have been very busy getting the word out and organizing things. While I was working, getting things going, it was easy to be totally dependent on God. Now that everything is ready to roll, I am facing a battle.

Today in my worship time, I was listening on my iPod to Matt Redmond's song "The Heart of Worship". I was singing along with it, as I often do, but when I got to the chorus, I changed the words of the song to say, "I'm coming back to the heart of 'ministry', it's all about you, all about you. I'm sorry Lord for the way I've made it, its all about you, all about you, Jesus".

So here is the question. Is what I am doing truly all about Him? Will He, and only He, receive the glory, or will I take some of it?

I am not sure that God is very worried about who gets the credit. I think He is worried about me. It is not right for me to depend on Him while laying the foundation for a ministry, and then, when all is ready, for me to take some credit for myself. Is my ministry all about Him, or is there a certain percentage in there for me?

Those of you who know me already know the answer. I am secretly wanting some of the glory. Yep, I do want the praise of men. These occasions give me the opportunity to see what I am really made of. Gold and silver are tried by fire and a man is tried by the praise he receives.[3]

Why is it so easy to depend on Him alone while I am ministering but when it is all over, I would like to get my grubby mitts on some of the glory? I have been in ministry for a while now and I should be over this, right?

So, I go to Him and I ask Him to please take this new ministry away from me. It is very possible that I will kill it if He lets me keep it. He does take it back from me. It is usually in my worship time that I give it to Him. That is the time that I am not really asking for anything, but I am just enjoying Him. He is so patient and understanding with me. I want Him to take back the ministry that He birthed

45

in me, that He developed in me and anointed me to carry out. I want Him to keep it. I can't claim any credit nor take any blame.

So I meditate on Jesus' words that ask how we can believe when we receive glory from one another.[4] Honestly God, right now I am guilty. I do believe it is all about You when I am depending on You to start a new ministry, but when I take some of the glory, I am guilty of wanting the praise of men.

Jesus, please make me more like the publican and less like the Pharisee.

1- John 12:43,

2- Luke 18:11

3- Proverbs 27:21

4- John 5:44

Security!

A few years ago, my brother-in-law Kepa and I rented some horses and went riding in the mountains between Madrid and Segovia, Spain. This is one of my favorite areas. We rode into the forest and all of a sudden we ran into some bulls; fighting bulls that are used in the bull ring! Alarmed, we stopped and watched for the reaction of the bulls. They lifted their heads and with an insulting disdain, continued eating. We were not a threat to them in any way. They paid no attention to us at all. They were, after all, fighting bulls and we were insignificant.

But on the other hand, a bull in the ring is insecure. He is put in a bull ring where there is a lot of noise from voices and trumpets and with a man who incessantly waves a cape in front of the bull's face. This is totally foreign to the bull's life experience and is very threatening. Under these circumstances, the bull attacks everything that moves.

When a bull feels secure, like in the forest that day with my brother-in-law, he is called, in bullfighting terms, meek. He feels no need to prove anything to anybody.

I want to be meek. Meekness is the result of feeling secure in who I am and who I am in God. The Lord Himself is our security.[1] I am secure under His wings.[2] "The work of righteousness shall be peace; and the effect of righteousness quietness and assurance for ever."[3]

If you do a search on the words 'confidence' or 'security', you will clearly see that God wants His children to be secure.

I am not at all impressed by a person who imposes his will on others, one who is compelled to use his bad temper whenever he perceives that he is not being respected. I am not impressed by someone who wants to receive recognition for what he has done or one who runs over everyone who gets in his way. This is not a person who is secure in who he is.

What does impress me is a person who can turn the other cheek when attacked, one who does not need to have his every good deed announced over a loudspeaker, and one who listens to those who are not in favor of his ideas without needing to reply. This person has the same spirit as Christ had.

Jesus said that we should learn of Him; for He **meek and lowly in heart.[4] There is no sign of humility or meekness in my flesh. I can not become meek by

47

making a list of the characteristics of a meek person and striving to incorporate those things into my life. The only way to become meek and humble is to learn — not from a book or from a teaching session, but to learn directly from Jesus. We need to spend time with Him as well as meditate on what the Bible tells us about Him. We need to be sensitive to the Spirit of whom Jesus said "...he shall receive of mine, and shall show it unto you."[5]

We can become truly meek and humble in heart. It is possible but it will never happen through our own efforts.

1- Psalms 71:5

2- Psalms 91:4

3- Isaiah 32:17

4- Matthew 11:29

5- John 16:14

Three Mistakes We Make

Although we are people who really want to please God, we still often commit three common errors. These arise because most of us are neither totally legalists nor do we totally walk in grace; we are a complicated combination of the two.

The first mistake we make is when we come to the conclusion that Christianity consists of 1) studying the Bible, 2) finding out what God wants and 3) dedicating ourselves to fulfilling His desires.

This little equation leaves out the intimate, personal relationship with our God. What I described in the last paragraph is a work-centered relationship much like that between an employee and his boss. The boss communicates what he wants to be done and the employee finds out what that entails and tries to do it to the best of his ability.

I am afraid that we teach this in our churches too often in spite of it being a very poor substitute for loving God will all our heart, soul, mind and strength.[1]

The second misunderstanding is similar to the first. We tend to fall into a daily routine, living our Christian lives based on principles.

I used to read three chapters of the Bible every day as a discipline. Once this obligation was fulfilled, I went on with my life. What I really needed out of my Bible reading was to touch God and to have Him touch me.

Reading to fulfill a commitment is very inferior to going to the Word of God to get closer to the Author.

Now when I read my Bible every morning, I do it to reestablish my intimate personal contact with God. My obligation is to meet with Him, not to complete a task. I read until it speaks to my soul; His Word is my schoolmaster that takes me to Him.[2]

The third error comes basically from believing a lie. We have a tendency to believe that what God wants is a holiness motivated by fear. There is nothing further from the truth. This lie give us an image of God that is nothing like what He is in reality.

If God wanted us to serve Him through fear, things would be much easier for Him. He would just have to show up and everybody everywhere would be terrified. In fact, He would only have to send an angel, for every time an angel

49

shows up in the Bible the first words the angel say is "Fear not".[3]

But it is not God's will that we live in fear. This is not what He wants, even though it would actually be easier for us to obey Him if this was His way of doing things.

What God wants more than anything else in this world is for us to love Him completely.[1] Because He wants this voluntary, sincere love from us, He has made things very complicated for Himself.

The Bible says that it is agape love, not fear, that produces the holiness and obedience that God seeks.[4]

We need a miracle. We need to be renewed in the spirit of our minds[5] until we have the mind of Christ.[6] We need to be changed; wonderfully transformed from glory to glory until His image is perfected in us.[7] Only then will we understand with our finite minds what God truly wants from us.

1- Matthew 22:37; Mark 12:30; Luke 10:27

2- Galatians 3:24

3- Luke 1:13, 30; Revelation 1:17, etc.

4- Matthew 22:40; Romans 13:10

5- Ephesians 4:23; Romans 12:2

6- 1 Corinthians 2:16

7- 2 Corinthians 3:18

Further Up and Further In (C.S. Lewis)

The legalist that lives in us has goals and dreams that are way too small to be from God. That is why we have to fight against the temptation to dream only of knowing the Bible and living a sin-free life. We have to go much further up and further in.

Obviously, all of us should know the Bible well. I am so glad that God did not give us His Word in the form of a theological work in 29 volumes. The Bible is small enough so that when we study and feed from it, we can get to know it well.

However, just knowing the Bible well is a goal that is too small. We need to go further in. The Scriptures testify about Jesus.[1] The Law is our schoolmaster that leads us to Christ[2] so our goal should be to know Jesus through the Bible. Isn't that what we tell the pre-Christians when we witness to them? We don't tell them they need to know the Bible, we tell them they need to know God. Jesus reaffirms that when He says that eternal life is to know the Father, the only true God and to know Jesus who was sent by the Father.[3] The legalist residing in us gets scared when he thinks of knowing God.

To live a sin-free life is also possible. But it is only possible when we are aiming at a much higher goal. Then we can achieve the intermediate goal.

Jesus does not want us to live in a defensive position. He doesn't want us to live in fear of contamination. He wants us to bravely launch out on the attack and to tread down our enemies.[4]

It is true that there are fiery darts shot our way by the enemy, but the shield of faith enables us to extinguish them all.[5] However this is still too small of a battle for a believer that has been baptized in the Spirit of Christ.

Our victory against sin, the world and the devil has already been won when we walk in the Spirit and do not satisfy the desires of the flesh.[6] We overcome the accuser by the blood of the Lamb, the word of our testimony and the fact that we don't love our lives even when we have to face death.[7] The victory is ours.

OK, but when someone talks like I am talking right now, we tend to think of a totally sinless life. I don't believe in a perfectly sinless life while we are here on earth, but I do believe and know from experience that we can consistently overcome because greater is He that is in us than he that is in the world.[8]

Jesus came to destroy the works of the enemy.[9] He specifically said that if we

51

believe, we will do greater works than He did when He was here on earth.[10] We are greater than John the Baptist[11] and by extension, the least of the Christians is greater than any man or woman in the Old Testament. Go ahead, say out loud with me, "I am greater than John the Baptist." It is true! The gates of hell do not stand a chance with us. Let's attack them and they will fall.

Let us not waste this abundant life that Jesus bought for us at such a high price. Every believer should be walking in and enjoying that abundant life of more than just a mere conqueror. Let's walk in faith and victory[12] and take it to the enemy.

1- John 5:39

2- Galatians 3:24

3- John 17:3,4

4- Psalms 60:12; 108:13

5- Ephesians 6:16

6- Romans 8:13; Galatians 5:16 (the original text for Galatians 5:16 that by walking in the Spirit, it will

follow automatically that we will not fulfill the lusts of the flesh.)

7- Revelation 12:11

8- 1John 4:4

9- 1John 3:8

10- John 14:12

11- Matthew 11:11

12- 1 John 5:4

The Hypocrite

I was the perfect hypocrite. I read the Bible every day, prayed for half an hour in tongues and half an hour in English, fasted one day a week, tithed, evangelized, and went to every service in my church.

Like many others who do all these things, I judged people. I compared them with myself and almost always believed that I was better. I was very proud-and one sign of pride is a bad temper.

I had a terrible one, and I'm ashamed to say that I took it out on the people around me.

A little girl prayed once, "God, please make the bad people good and the good people nice."

I thought that reading the Bible, praying and going to church would help me become a better person, that they would take away my selfishness and anger.

They didn't, though.

This is totally understandable. Who prayed more than the Pharisees? Who fasted more than them or knew the Scriptures more? Nobody. In spite of their overt 'devotion', they were the ones who received the most severe chewing-out from Jesus. On one occasion He said to them, "Woe unto you, Pharisees! for you tithe mint and rue and all manner of herbs, and pass over justice and the love of God: these you ought to have done, and not to leave the other undone." [1]

Prayer, fasting and going to church did not make me better. I was guilty of being faithful in some things and very deficient in others; important things like justice and love.

Back then I treated my sin problem in a very legalistic way. I fought to overcome it and in so doing guaranteed failure. The only one that could make me better was Jesus.

These days I still pray, fast and go to church, but not because I'm hoping they'll make me a better person. I do them because they help me get closer to Jesus.

In 1771, an Englishman named John Berridge wrote a letter to John Newton (the author of "Amazing Grace"). He told him we have to submit ourselves to the righteousness of Christ and that it is not our righteousness but Christ 's that is going to save us.

Not long ago, one of my best friends asked me, "We know we have to be holy, but how do we become holy? Is it by striving or by resting?" The answer, of course, is through rest- or as John Berridge said, by submission to Christ's righteousness.

There is no other remedy for sin. Jesus is my righteousness and I have to submit to Him.[2] He is my justification, sanctification and redemption. There is no hope outside of Him.[3]

When I see selfishness and bad temper lift their ugly heads in me, I remember a song "In the Light" by DC Talk, a famous Christian band from last century: "What's going on inside me? I despise my own behavior. This only serves to confirm my suspicions that I am still a man in need of a Savior."

1- Luke 11:42

2- Romans 6:19

3- 1 Timothy 1:1

When I Grow Up

I read an article a few years ago that chilled me to the core. It said that the majority of the pastors in the United States stop growing spiritually when they are about 45 years old. (How do they know this stuff?) It seems that pastors learn to do a job — how to counsel, to preach, to administrate a church, etc. and because they really don't need to learn much more, they put it on cruise control and continue until they retire.

The reason it chilled me is because I am no better. With all that I have to do, I am not looking for more work here.

It would be easy to fall into that trap. But I have made four goals for myself in order to avoid the trap. In this chapter, I am going to talk about two of them and in the next one, the other two.

1) I need to know God. That is what eternal life is according to John 17:3. God has always wanted us to know Him. He made us in His image so we could understand Him.

Knowing God was Paul's passion.[1] And the worst words we could ever hear would be if Jesus said to us to depart because He never knew us.[2]

Now I am not talking about knowing more about Him — many of us have made Christianity a moral philosophy to be mentally assented to. No, I want to know Him.

To know Him I have to spend time with Him. I am not just referring to time in prayer — people from every religion pray — but to something much deeper. It is relating to Him.

I have to keep my heart sensitive if I am to hear His still, small voice. A hardened heart is a deaf heart. I am way over those 45 years of age. I need to be teachable.

2) I need to be humble. I am not sure I really understand what humility is. Sometimes we think that we have to put ourselves down to be humble. Our example of humility is Jesus. He did not go around talking bad about Himself. He told us that without Him we could do nothing.[3] That can sound like bragging. But He also instructed people not to tell anyone about the healing they had just received.[4] He deflected the credit often, saying things like their faith had healed them.[5]

55

I have two major problems in my desire to be truly humble. 1) I don't really know what true humility is unless God reveals it to me. The mysteries of God are not understood or learned, they are revealed. 2) I can't become more humble without help. Marisa helps me in this. Life and its unfairness does, too. They show me where I am being proud. (Just about every time I find myself irritable, it can be traced back to pride.)

Jesus, seeing my fruitless struggle to reform, tells me to go to Him, to learn from Him because he is meek and humble down in His heart. He said that if I achieve humility, I will find rest for my soul.[6] True humility brings rest for the soul!

Paul did not want anyone to think more of him than what they saw or heard from him.[7] He did not tell us about some of his experiences because it would make people admire him more. (We, on the other hand, tend to hide things that would make people think less of us.) Paul gloried in his weaknesses[8] and tried to hide his achievements.[7] God exalts[9] and gives grace[10] to the humble. I want to be truly humble.

Jesus ran away from those who wanted to crown Him king.[11] Paul hid some of the high points of his faith to avoid looking too good![7]

There is something I often say that helps me to put it all in perspective:

"Due to circumstances out of my control... things are going well!"

1- Philippians 3:10

2- Matthew 7:23

3- John 15:5

4- Matthew 8:4; Mark 1:44; 8:26

5- Matthew 9:22, Mark 5:34; 10:52; Luke 7:50; 8:48; 17:19; 18:42

6- Matthew 11:29

7- 2 Corinthians 12:6

8- 1 Corinthians 12:5, 9 & 10

9- James 4:10; 1 Peter 5:6

10- James 4:6; 1 Peter 5:5

11- John 6:15

When I Grow Up... Part 2

3) I want to be grateful.

A grateful person generally is humble. One of the things I use to crush my pride is expressing gratitude out loud for things someone does for me.

As a minister (servant) we of all people should be most grateful. If any good comes out of my ministry, whether it is from my preaching, my counseling, teaching or even finding guidance that I need for my life, it is a miracle of God. There is a verse that says 'unless the Lord builds the house, the workers labor in vain.'[1] This is so true!

Rick Joyner once said that if a pastor thinks that he deserves the applause of the people, that is like the donkey that carried Jesus in the Triumphal Entry thinking that the 'hosannas' were for him.

But it gets even worse. When we ministers allow ourselves to receive the praise, we become thieves. We are taking something that is not ours. Let's not fool ourselves. We are stealing something that belongs only to God.

Gratitude for something that God or another person has done for us comes from a humble heart. In order to truly thank someone, we first have to recognize that we are not self-sufficient nor independent and that we need a helping hand.

Expressing gratitude to others is hard on our pride. Why is it so hard, especially when it has to do with the people we love the most? All of us like it when someone acknowledges an extra effort that we exert.

I want to be known in heaven and on earth as a grateful person.

4) I want to be fruitful.

This is another miracle. I can do works, but to produce fruit means I have to be grafted into the vine.[2] If His vigor is not running through my veins, I cannot produce fruit.

The number one thing He wants from me and my life is the fruit of the Spirit. The verse in Ephesians 5 says that the fruit of the Spirit is in all goodness, righteousness and truth. These are not an easy combination to find in a person - goodness, righteousness and truth. There are times that I lean more toward righteousness and truth and become exacting but then there is not very much

57

goodness around. Other times I can have lots of goodness but have to make sure it is not at the cost of righteousness and truth. God wants me to have all three and so do I.

For me to have the fruit of the Spirit depends much more on the Spirit than on me— it is after all His fruit. I just have to be grafted into the vine[3] and if there is a healthy, consistent relationship with Him, His fruit will be in my life.

On the other hand, if His fruit is not in my life, it is because I don't have that healthy, consistent relationship with Him. Easy, isn't it? For all my striving, I can not produce love, joy, peace, patience, kindness, goodness, faithfulness, gentleness or self-control.[4] This is not like a breakfast buffet where you pick and choose what you want We need to have all of them in our lives.

I want to be that kind of person. If I have the fruit of the Spirit then I will for sure produce other types of fruit for God — souls getting saved, bodies being healed, the afflicted being comforted and the captives set free.

To know God, to be humble, to be grateful and to bear fruit. These goals for my life are out of my reach, but through Christ, I can do all things.[5]

1- Psalms 127:1

2- John 15:4,5

3- John 15:5, 8

4- Galatians 5:22, 23

5- Philippians 4:13

58

Jesus Loves Me!

I have talked in this book about the supreme importance of love, and how love makes the Christian life not only possible but also easy to live. In this chapter I would like to reflect on the love God has for you.

Lately I see a lot of people that worry about what God thinks of them. Not only that, but some of the people that have these worries seem convinced that they have let God down big time and that God is not happy with them at all.

My first conclusion when I observe this is that I am talking with a sincere person. The insincere "hope" that God understands them and that He knows that boys will be boys all the while their hearts are hardened.

So, sincere people want to please God. The problem comes in when they see Him like the servant in the parable saw Him, as a "hard man" who is never satisfied and always pushing for more.[1] This is a legalistic point of view. What? God loves the sinners, but we Christians have to win His love on a daily basis?

That is a lie of the devil.

It is true that God wants us to love Him with all our heart, soul, mind and strength,[2]

But it is also true that God loves you with all His heart, all His soul, all His mind and all His strength. He is madly in love with you.[3]

Zephaniah 3:17 says, "The LORD thy God in the midst of thee is mighty; he will save, he will rejoice over thee with joy; he will rest in his love, he will joy over thee with singing." So, let me see. He rejoices, He sings and He rests in His love. He really, really loves you.

You might object, "Well, yeah God showed His love for us because while we were yet sinners Christ died for us.[4] But now that we are His sons, He is much more demanding, isn't He?"

Uhmmm…no!

"Behold, what manner of love the Father has given us, that we should be called the sons of God..."[5] "And we have known and believed the love that God feels for us. God is love; and he that lives in love lives in God, and God in him."[6]

How many times are we called beloved in the Epistles? (pssst — 34 times and once he calls us "dearly beloved"[7]). Do a search in your Bible program for the word "beloved" in the Epistles. It will do you good.

If a human father were like what we imagine God to be like, (demanding, never satisfied, exacting) that earthly father would be a terrible father and his kids would likely have personal problems.

In Psalms 103:13, 14 we read, "As a father pities his children, so the LORD has pity on them that fear him. He knows our frame; he remembers that we are dust."

A few years ago a friend told me, "My daughter is my best friend. I love her. Of course every once in a while I have to be a mother, but every time I have to, my desire is to go back to being friends as soon as possible."

God enjoys you.[8] Of course He has to carry out His fatherly duties every once in a while, but He does it with the happy expectation of relating to you again as a friend.

1- Matthew 25:14-30

2- Luke 10:27

3- John 3:16

4- Romans 5:8

5- 1 John 3:1

6- 1 John 4:16

7- 2 Corinthians 12:19

8- Song of Solomon chapter 2

Don't Stress

In 1978 I worked as a cook at an all-night restaurant along I-5 in Red Bluff, CA. One morning around 7:30, I was headed home on my bicycle when I saw a man who was already drunk, sitting on the stairs in front of the post office. Suddenly, the word of the Lord came to me saying, "Go and tell him that I love him."

So, naturally, I began to argue with God, giving Him every reason I could think of why I shouldn't do what He asked of me. "I am very uncomfortable with this, Jesus," I told Him. "I don't know this man. Besides, he is going to think all your children are fanatics if I just walk up to him and tell him You love him. I don't think that is the image you want to give him. So for your own sake, Lord, I am going to have to tell you 'no' on this one."

I kept pedaling down the street. I was not struck by lightening. God did not take my name out of His book as He does not obligate us to do that which is right. He respects our free will.

Grace is much less stressful than legalism. It is better for our health, both for those of us in spiritual leadership and also for those who work with us in the church.

I did go back that morning in 1978 to where the drunken man was sitting and I did witness to him. But this does not indicate that God did not give me the freedom to make a mistake, to refuse to obey, or even to rebel. It even goes further. Through His grace, He has already provided for my repentance[1] and for His forgiveness.[2]

I just read a secular biology book. I enjoy reading science books. One of the chapters dealt with biology and stress. Stress is such a plague in our generation that there have been numerous studies done on it from every angle. One study showed that if you give two groups of people the same task, the group which is given strict directions and deadlines will experience far more elevated blood pressure and a marked increase in stress hormones than the other.

There are many factors that exert pressure on us— things that limit our options when we have to make decisions. For example, genetics. I have a personality that is much like my mother's. This conditions how I approach stressful situations. I have many responsibilities to fulfill and the demands of my job. Then there are my family's needs. Socially I have a group of friends that I want to like me. And let's not forget that the clock is ticking, that my health could fail and that my resources are limited. Many things exert pressure on me every day.

We in positions of spiritual leadership can add to people's stressors using things like guilt, shame or intimidation. When we do this, we are being very unfair to those who are under our spiritual care. It is a sin for spiritual leadership to coerce people in order to "help" them do the right thing or by forcing them to avoid making mistakes.

1- Romans 2:4; 2 Corinthians 7:10

2- Ephesians 1:7; James 5:5; 1 John 1:9

62

Hunger and Thirst

When I read some of the Psalms that say things like "as the deer pants after the water brooks so my soul pants after you"[1] or like "God you are my God, early will I seek you, my soul thirsts for you and my flesh longs for you like it was a dry and thirsty land where no water was",[2]

I realize I still have not arrived at that level. I love God's ways, His Word and His work. But when I compare my desire to know Him more and what I read in these Psalms, ●●●●●●●●●● am light-years away.

When I gave my life to the Lord, what I wanted was that "intimate and personal relationship" with Him. The joy that I felt in getting to know Him, and being able to hear Him, was incredible. For the first time in my life I was really happy. I finally experienced gladness and peace.

But more than anything else, what I felt was joy, an unspeakable joy.[3]

But some things came up that started to take Jesus' place in my life. They were good things, like His ways, His work, or His Word. But they became goals to achieve rather than tools or fruit of being in love with Him with all my heart soul, mind and strength.

My Christian life had become more and more difficult and my joy faded.

I know God.[4] I feel Him in my life. He speaks to me. This relationship is an incredible part of my life every day.

But when I see those verses in Psalms 42 or 63 and I compare the desire that the Psalmists felt and the desire I feel (and remember they had not even been born again, they had not been baptized in the Holy Spirit, they did not have access to the New Testament — they didn't even have the Psalms to read, they were writing them!)

I see that I really don't measure up to them in desire.

When the psalmist talks about thirsting in a dry and thirsty land, he is talking about a constant felt need. When you are out in the desert for several hours without water, you don't think of anything else except quenching your thirst.

So, I am asking God to give me that which I do not have — this hunger and thirst. I need Him more. I live to see Him. I am dying to see Him.

I could ask to know Him more and He would give it to me. But I want something a bit more consistent. So I am asking for hunger; a deep, deep hunger, and for thirst; thirst like a man in the desert. I want this desire to fill my thoughts.

I'll let you know how it's going.

1- Psalm 42:1

2- Psalm 63:1

3- 1 Peter 1:8

4- John 1:18

Two Prodigals

The legalist that is in all of us believes that we have to earn God's favor. We might never say it out loud, but our tendency is to feel like this. The two sons in the parable of the Prodigal Son also had that mentality.

The first son, the Bible says, went to a far land in a distant province and there squandered his money on wild living.[1] A while later, while he was feeding pigs, he reflected on his sad state, the result of his own choices. He came to the logical conclusion that he did not deserve anything from his father. He had wasted all his opportunities and had done it knowingly. He had nothing to offer. If he had a little money, he might have been able to invest it and go home with as much or more than he had when he left. Sure, his life had been shameful in every way, but at least he would not return home empty handed.

So he figured that he had forever lost his privileged position as a son. He decided to ask his father for a job, the only possibility left for someone who had been such an idiot for so long a time, someone who had "spent everything".[2] Even so, it was not a sure thing that his father would give him a job. He had been so irresponsible that he did not deserve anyone's trust at all.

The other son reacted when he saw his father extend unmerited grace. (Yeah, yeah, I know that grace is unmerited favor, but this is unmerited grace!) Grace is only given to those who do not deserve it.

The legalistic mindset made the older brother react against that unmerited grace that his father showed. He saw an extraordinary love and forgiveness and he was offended. He had worked there for a lot of years and had "never disobeyed". He now reproached his Father saying "you have never even given me a kid goat to have a party with my friends. Then this jerk of a kid of yours who has wasted all your hard-earned money on harlots comes home and you don't kill a goat, you kill the fatted calf!" [3] He didn't want to see a party. He wanted to see punishment.

He felt that he deserved the blessings of his father more than his brother because he had "never disobeyed". He was a better son. The other had been despicable and spent half of the estate on prostitutes. It would have been incredible grace to let him back into the family, but to also throw him a party was way overboard.

The father's answer to the older son shows us both the heart of the father as well as the error of the son. The elder son's way of thinking (and it is our way of thinking, too) was wrong. He did not have to earn the right to have a party with his friends. He could have any party he wanted. He not only could have killed the fatted calf for his party and his friends, he could have killed off the whole herd for it was his. We do not have to earn that which is already ours by birthright. We are sons and daughters.

Let us get rid of this legalistic mindset. There is nothing we can do to make God love us more and there is nothing we can do to make Him love us less. He is not interested in the kind of relationship that depends on our behavior. (Our behavior, even on our very best day, would not cut it.) We are His children. He loves us just as we are. He has given everything to us, not because we have been so exemplary, but because we are His children and He loves us.

So, let's love Him back. Let's not be motivated by what we can get out of the relationship with Him. Let our desire be to see Him smile, to make Him happy•• •ecause we love Him.

1- Luke 15:13

2- Luke 15:14

3- Luke 15:29, 30

The Easy Way

In his book "What's so Amazing about Grace?", Philip Yancy illustrates a point by referring to some German classes he had to take one summer. He wondered what would have happened if the registrar had come up to him and said, "Philip, we want you to study hard, learn German and take the test, but we promise you in advance that you'll get a passing grade. Your diploma has already been filled out."

If that was the case, would he have spent every moment of that summer studying German verbs?

Without the threat of a bad grade, how could the registrar expect any students to apply themselves? Knowing how we are, which of us would study diligently if we knew we were going to pass the class anyway?

God has promised us forgiveness. Grace assures us that we will be forgiven and approved, whatever our sins may be, if we repent and ask forgiveness with all our heart.[1] Forgiveness is ours after a sincere request.

Exodus 34: 6,7 describes God as "...merciful and gracious, longsuffering, and abundant in goodness and truth, keeping mercy for thousands, forgiving iniquity and transgression and sin."A large percentage of what is written in the books in the Pentateuch is dedicated to how we get forgiven by God. He wants to forgive. Every moment of every day, that is His desire.

But...doesn't that open things up for us to take advantage of grace?

Of course it does! I myself have taken advantage and abused the goodness of God. What else can you expect if He so willing to forgive all the time?

On the other hand, since there is no threat of reaching the limits of God's grace, how can God expect us to fulfill our duty without taking advantage of and abusing His infinite patience?

Yancey affirms that if there is no threat of a failing grade, very few of us would study as we should. So what can motivate students to apply themselves sufficiently?

He says they will make the effort to learn German if they fall in love with a German. True love does not need the threat of punishment to motivate a person to do even the most difficult things. I know this is true from personal experience.

After knowing Marisa (and falling head over heels in love with her) I had to go back to California and get a job. It took eight months to earn enough to go back to Spain where she was running a Teen Challenge coffee house.

During this time I had no problem being faithful to her. I wrote her 180 letters in those eight months. (This was long before email). I called her on the phone as often as I could. All of these things- and a few gifts that I sent her, too- did not require any sacrifice on my part. I was in love.

You could say that those letters I wrote her could be compared to our daily time in the Word; it is not a chore to communicate with someone you are in love with. Along the same lines, my phone calls could be compared to our time in prayer. I wanted to be able to talk to Marisa and therefore it was easy for me to write so many letters and call her on the phone. Being faithful was not hard at all, just like it is not hard for a Christian in love to avoid sin. According to 2 Corinthians 5:14, the love of Christ constrains us.

Love fulfills the law.[2] His commandments are not grievous.[3] His yoke is easy and his burden is light.[4] This is so true if we love Him with all our heart, soul, mind and strength.[5] This is not just a commandment•it is the key to the Christian life. Loving God and loving your neighbor not only make Christianity possible, they make it easy.

Jude tells us in verse 21 that we need to keep ourselves in the love of God and look for the mercy of Jesus unto eternal life.

1- Matthew 21:31

2- Romans 13:10

3- 1 John 5:3

4- Matthew 11:30

5- Mark 12:30; Luke 10:27

What do I Know?

One Sunday after church, I was sitting in our living room in my recliner. One of the young men from church was with us that afternoon and all my effort was concentrated on not falling asleep. This young man — Antonio — was one of the leaders in the youth group. He was very active in street ministry and had been baptized in water. All of a sudden, he looked at me and said, "You're very intimidating!"

I used to go to a café in town here to have a cup of expresso and read my Bible. I would sit at a table away from everyone else and read the Word. The owner's daughter was working one morning. She was about 22 years old at that time and was sleeping with her boyfriend. While I was reading, she came up to my table and told me, "Every time you come in here there is such an incredible peace."

What is going on here?

What do I know? If in that moment you had asked me, I would have told you that Antonio needed to be encouraged, that he needed to be recognized for what he was doing. However, the Spirit decided that afternoon to get serious with him. It turns out that Antonio was thinking about leaving his faith and his Lord and going back to the world. Antonio did not need encouragement nor my recognition. The Spirit knew that, I didn't.

As far as the young woman in the café, I would have rebuked her and warned her about her eternal future if she did not change the way she was living. But the Spirit knows much more than I do. She later told me that she had been raped when she was 12 and every day she thought of suicide. The Spirit knew that she needed peace and He Himself gave it to her.

Wherever I go, I try to be very sensitive to the Spirit. But in order to be sensitive to Him, I need enough humility to know that I have no clue about what is going on around me spiritually. When I avoid judging by the outside and coming to my own conclusions, He can work through me.

Sometimes He tells me what I need to do. Other times, as in Antonio's case and with the young woman in the café, I just see what He is doing and try not to mess it up. I have to openly recognize that I don't have the slightest idea of what He is doing unless He reveals it to me.

When He was talking to the Samaritan woman, Jesus told her straight out that He was the Messiah.[1] This was one of the very few times in the Gospels that He

69

said that in so many words. He did not rebuke her, because she did not need rebuking. On another occasion, Peter, one of Jesus' best, most intimate friends, did need a rebuke and he got one of the severest ones in the whole Bible.[2]

We need to be sensitive to the Spirit. The Pharisees had automatic responses for almost every possible situation. They had worked out a system where (to paraphrase Newton) every action received an equal and opposite reaction. This works in science. Working with people, we don't need science, we need art, the art of the Spirit.

1- John 4:26

2- Matthew 16:23

I'm Drowning!

We need to take very seriously the verses in Proverbs that say, "Trust in the LORD with all thine heart; and lean not unto thine own understanding. In all thy ways acknowledge him, and he shall direct thy paths. Be not wise in thine own eyes"[1]

I make goofy comments about my need to "get saved" every morning but I just wonder, when He says that His "mercies are new every morning*" doesn't that indicate that I need His mercies every morning?

It is extremely important that I start every day getting in tune with the Spirit. I have no idea what is awaiting me every day and even less of an idea of what God has in mind for me that day.

I could just live another day of my life by inertia (and who knows how many more days I have in this life) or I can live every one of my days with purpose and meaning as the Spirit guides.

There is no doubt that I have far fewer years left for ministry ahead of me than I have behind me.

Over time, you acquire experience in ministry. I have been able to read a mountain of books and have been discipled by men and women of God.

But if I understand fully what I need to do, if I can do it myself, if I can control the situation, than it is much too small to be of God.

I want to be in way over my head in deep water. I want my task to be so huge that I can not control it. If I can touch bottom and get my nose above water, then the water is not nearly deep enough.

I believe that those of you who have read this far know how I think. Even so, I feel that I need to emphasize that I am not talking about dumbing down Christianity.

It is just that I don't want to waste my days on projects that are within my abilities. I don't want to waste my days on stupid stuff, either. The fact that something is impossible does not necessarily mean that it is God. What I need is for Him to guide me and for me to follow His leading.

So I wait on Him. I need to hear His voice every day. I need to be sensitive to

His Spirit. I don't even write an email until I spend time in the morning with Him — both in His word and in prayer. It is like I get spiritually dressed first and then I go to work.

His thoughts are much, much higher than my thoughts. His ways are really higher than my ways. The difference is like that of heaven and earth.[3] His thoughts and ways are light-years ahead, literally.

The ways I want to walk in are His ways.

1- Proverbs 3:5-7

2- Lamentations 3:23

3- Isaiah 55:8, 9

The Word and the Rest

In Hebrews chapters 3 and 4, where the author goes deeply into how to rest in God, he gives us three tools at the end of the discourse. To enter into the rest is the opposite of legalism which is works based.

When we enter into the rest, accoring to Hebrews 4:10, we cease from our own works. In place of our own works, we start walking in the works that God has prepared for us beforehand.[1] The Spirit initiates the works, He guides us as to how and when to do them and He finishes them • It is the Spirit at work in us.

Hebrews 4:11 affirms that not to enter into the rest is "disobedience". But to get to the place where we relax and let the river of God carry us, we need help. That is why the Scriptures not only warn us about the severe consequences[2] of not entering into the divine rest, it also give us the three tools[3] that have been prepared to help us to enter in and live in His rest.

The first tool is the Word.[4] The Word of God is a foundational help for our Christian life. It is solid and never changing.[5] When everything around us is relative and circumstantial, the Word of God is a rock under our feet.

Hebrews 4:12 tells us that it is powerful and cuts better than any two-edged sword. It gets right down to the soul and the spirit, the joints and the marrow and it discerns the thoughts and intents of our heart.

According to that text in Hebrews, one job of the Word is to expose our heart so we can see it just as it is. This is very important. My heart, according to Jeremiah 17:9 is deceitful above all things, and, to top it all off, desperately wicked. My heart deceives me constantly.

One of the main tools that God uses to let me see what is in my heart is the Word. The Word penetrates so deep it differentiates the soul and the spirit in me and it discerns the (deceitful) thoughts and intents of my heart.

I think all of us have gone through the following: we believe that we are doing God's will, but it turns out to be a dead work![6] A dead work that was not initiated by the Spirit, that the Spirit is not directing and that the Spirit is not going to finish for me. Whatever I start is up to me to finish, God is not going to do it. But if the Spirit starts it, He will guide it and He will finish it through me.

So the Word penetrates my life, separates my soul — my mind, will and emotions — from my spirit or the part of me that communes with God.[4] All of a

73

sudden I realize that my dead work was fruit of my soul and not something that God planted in my spirit. Everything is naked and exposed.[4] I have been found out by the Word.

In that moment, what I need to do is to repent.[6] I need to get rid of the dead works that rob me of my time and my energy. The Word penetrates my heart, I am no longer deceived but rather naked and exposed.[4]

And now I can see that the dead work that I initiated myself, is taking the place of another work, an incredible work that God prepared beforehand for me to walk in.[1]

In the next chapter we will talk about the Great High Priest[7] and how He helps us to escape a works-based Christianity and enter into the rest that God gives us when His Spirit guides.

1- Ephesians 2:10

2- Hebrews 3:8-13; 4:1, 11

3- Hebrews 4:11-16

4- Hebrews 4:12,13

5- Matthew 5:18; Luke 16:17; 1 Peter 1:25

6- Hebrews 6:1

7- Hebrews 4:15

The High Priest and the Rest

God desires that we enter into His rest and has provided everything that we could need- forgiveness of our iniquities, freedom from the slavery of sin, divine healing (physical, mental or emotional).

Our High Priest, Jesus, lived His whole life in God's rest. He did nothing on His own initiative, but only that which His Father told Him.[1] He, through His Spirit, wants to guide us to enter into that rest.

A good friend of mine called me one day on the phone. He was all worked up. He was in the process of entering into the rest and he had seen the rest which was at work in Jesus' life. He was amazed. Jesus did not go around the earth grabbing onto people and forcing them to avoid hell- and Jesus knew better than anyone what hell was really like.

Jesus just did what His Father told him. He did not react to the need. Rather, He followed the leading of God.

Everything Jesus did, He did in submission to the Holy Spirit, just like you and I need to do![1] And living like this, He showed us the amazing things that God can do. He showed us what a man or a woman that is submitted to God can achieve.[2]

Our Great High Priest knows very well what life down here is like and what it can be like if we live it in the Spirit. If Jesus preferred to live submitted to His Father's will, it was because living is better that way.

This is why he was able to pass by the pool of Bethesda and reach out to heal only one of the many people there needing healing.[3] He surely must have gone many, many times by the Gate Beautiful in the Temple, but healing the lame man that was begging there would be Peter's task in a few months.[4] He did not react to the need, He followed the leading of God.

As it says in the last part of Hebrews chapter 4, our High Priest has done absolutely everything necessary to help us to enter into His rest. This is His desire. He is insistent that each one of us enter into the rest.[5]

He sat down at the right hand of the throne in heaven.[6] He has everything under control. He has years of experience. He knows very well what He is doing. God never panics. And this is what He wants life to be like on earth, too. It is a pretty lame testimony to say, "Be a born-again Christian and stressed like me".

This rest from God sure sounds good. But our mentality in the 21st century insists that we are not responsible citizens unless we live stressed out. We need these verses about the rest at the end of this chapter in Hebrews that tell us to labor to enter into that rest and that they that enter God's rest cease from their own works just as God did from His. Only when we cease from our own works will He begin to do His works through us.

Jesus was tempted to do things in His own strength, even by his own friends and family.[7] But He didn't do them. He was obedient to God, submitted to God, and above all, living in God's rest. Being stressed out or fried is not a characteristic of good, productive Christians.

1- John 14:10

2- John 5:1-8

3- John 14:12

4- Acts 3:10

5- Hebrews 4:1

6- Mark 16:19

7- John 7:3-5, Matthew 16:21-23

Full Access

Access to the Throne of God. That is the whole point. We have seen how God uses the Word to help us enter into His rest. In another chapter, using the same text in Hebrews 4 we talked about our Great High Priest whose name is Love, and how He helps us to rest in God. In this chapter, we will examine how through the ministry of the Bible and that of Jesus to us, • •• ••• •• •••••• the Throne of Grace.

God is not looking for us to be stressed. He is not impressed when we burn out or get exhausted. That has never been His will for our lives. He has provided His Word which is sharper than a two-edged sword, discern•• ••the thoughts and intentions of our hearts,[1] and shows • •••••• ••• •••• we are still urgently in need •••••••••••••

So then He provided the Savior. The Savior, in His position as the Great High Priest, has compassion on our weaknesses and prepares a way for us by offering the needed sacrifice — Himself.[2]

We must not live the Christian life through our own strength. This is the legalists' error. They are sincere, but try as they might, if they don't wait on the Lord, they will never rise up on wings of eagles, nor run and not be weary nor walk and not faint.[3]

So, the "new and living way" He opened up for us[4] really exists. The key is to boldly go to the Throne of Grace to get mercy and grace in our times of need.[5]

When you are stressed, go to the Throne of Grace. When circumstances are overwhelming you, go to the Throne of Grace. When you have problems, go to the Throne of Grace to receive help in your time of need. To sum it up, when I see that I am overwhelmed, in deep confusion or anxiety, it is a sign — I need to go to the Throne of Grace.

Paul commanded us to not be anxious about anything![6] Come on, Paul. This is the 21st century. We live in the age of stress. This 'not being anxious about anything' sounds really good, but it doesn't work in our day and age.

What is the solution that Paul gives us? When we are anxious about something. pray! Go to the Throne of Grace and get help.[5]

You are not alone. You don't have to face anything at all alone. You can always call on Jesus. At any time, in any circumstance, in any place. He wants you to live with an illogical peace, one that does not make sense.[7] And it is truly easy.[8]

That is why Hebrews 4:1 warns us that we should fear. There is still a promise of entering into His rest. Don't let it be that any one of us seem to come short of it. Very few times are we exhorted in the Bible to fear but this is one of them.

He has arranged everything. It is all within your reach. You don't have to go up to heaven to get it nor do you have to go way down in the deep. It is in your mouth and in your heart.[9]

But, if we insist on living the Christian life and try to obtain the holiness He requires[10] by our own striving, then we should be afraid. Don't do it. Go to the Throne of Grace.

1- Hebrews 4:12

2- Hebrews 4:14, 15; 9:14

3- Isaiah 40:31

4- Hebrews 10:20

5- Hebrews 4:16

6- Philippians 4:6

7- Philippians 4:7

8- Matthew 11:30

9- Romans 10:6-8

10- Hebrews 12:14

Can't Get There from Here

One year when Marisa and I were itinerating, visiting churches in California to report on our work in Spain, we arrived for a service in a small town in the Central Valley. We asked a man on the street where we could find the Assembly of God church. He assured us that he knew where it was but in all seriousness said, "You can't get there from here." He repeated that several times. So I then asked him, "Is there some place around here that we can go to and from there get to the church?" "Yes!" he said and pointed out a small market and from the market it was easy to get to the church.

Obviously, talking from a geographical point of view, it is a silly response. Even if we were in China we could eventually arrive at the church in that town. It would cost money and time, but we could arrive.

Spiritually, however, that statement makes sense.

Everything I need for my life and ministry is beyond my reach. My efforts to get what I need have been spectacular failures.

One example is if I need peace, even though I make all efforts, even if I tell myself to "chill out", I can not enjoy the peace that I need. Perfect peace comes to those whose mind is stayed on God: because they trust in God.[1] Instead of striving to get the result I need, I have to concentrate on that which is going to produce the desired result. Peace that passes all understanding does not come from my own efforts, it comes from not being anxious and from praying with thanksgiving.[2]

The same can be said about spiritual strength. Living the life that God expects from us requires spiritual strength. Our natural tendency is to strive. But Biblically, renewed strength comes from waiting on the Lord.[3] We don't even need to go on vacation to renew our strength (and I love vacation).

I need self control to be able to serve Him. But self control is not a part of my personality. It is a fruit of the Spirit.[4]

Holiness is something that God requires.[5] • •have an innate tendency to think that•yeah, salvation is by faith but after that I have to live out the Christian life — of course, with Jesus' help. I tried this and ended up spiritually exhausted.

Galatians speaks about those that believe that salvation is by faith but afterward strive in themselves to be holy and to please God with their works.

79

My works are still filthy rags.[6] They are "christian" (with a small "c") filthy rags, but they are still filthy rags. According to Romans 10:3, this is a direct result of our ignorance. "For they being ignorant of God's righteousness, and going about to establish their own righteousness, have not submitted themselves unto the righteousness of God." I have to submit to God's righteousness.

Should I go on? Where does the anointing that I need so badly come from? Where do I get my guidance? What about the power I need, or the discernment, or the Agape love? I desperately need them but cannot produce them myself. I can't get there from here.

It doesn't depend on me. It is impossible to live the life that God expects from me. Yet, if I submit to God, through faith in Him, "all things that pertain unto life and godliness" are given to me through His divine power.[7]

The difference between doing it in my own strength and letting God do it through me is the difference between works and fruit.

1- Isaiah 26:3

2- Philippians 4:6,7

3- Isaiah 40:31

4- Galatians 5:23

5- 1 Peter 1:16

6- Isaiah 64:6

7- 2 Peter 1:3

The Slavery of Success

One of the main problems in our fight against legalism is knowing how to identify it. I do not believe that anyone who has made it this far in this book is a total legalist. I also do not believe that anyone in history has been totally free of legalism — except, of course, for Jesus Christ. The rest of us seem to have a mixture of legalism and learning to live by grace in various areas of our lives. The big advantage we have is that we are aware of our legalistic tendencies and we fight to eliminate them.

One huge characteristic of life in this 21st century is that of striving to achieve success.

The disciples of John the Baptist were worried.[1] Up until then it seemed like John had exclusive rights to the revival. He had achieved a lot of success in ministry. The Bible informs us that all of Judea and all the people of Jerusalem were going out to him.[2] Then a new guy — his cousin — had set up a competing campaign. This new evangelistic campaign was stealing John's sheep!

John was not a slave of success. He had tasted it and had enjoyed it for a time, but he was not its slave. That is why he could say those very famous words, " He must increase, but I must decrease."[3]

It doesn't seem that numbers were very important to Jesus either. I am reminded of two times that Jesus had great multitudes listening to him and all of a sudden He did things that guaranteed his numerical implosion. In the first occasion he left a growing revival to cross the lake and attend to one demon-possessed man who lived in a cemetary.[4] In the other occasion he gave a word that confused people (and even grossed them out) when he said they had to eat His flesh and drink His blood.[5] Kind of sounds like cannibalism! Everybody left Him.

When Marisa and I started a church in a small town near Madrid, things were going slowly. We had service every day except Monday. We invited a lot of people to the meetings but nobody showed up. We handed out a lot of tracts with the church's address but for the first seven weeks no one came. Marisa would lead me in worship and I would preach to her. Nobody came this whole time. We found ourselves fighting disappointment and discouragement.

One day I received a word from the Lord for my life. He told me that if the lack of people depressed me then when large numbers of people began to come it would go right to my head. I needed to follow Him only.

81

There was a teen who went into a coffee shop to make a phone call on the pay phone. As the owner of the coffee shop listened in, the young man said, "Mr. Jones? Good. I would like to ask you if you need help in your shop. .. Oh, you already have someone? OK, can I ask you if you are happy with him?... You are. Good, OK, well thanks, Mr. Jones. Have a good afternoon. Bye." The owner of the coffee shop said to the boy, "Are you looking for work? I need someone around here." "No, thank you, sir" the teen said, "I already work for Mr. Jones." "What? Then what was that whole conversation about with Mr. Jones?" "Well," the young man said, "I just wanted to know if he was happy with my work."

Let's be sensitive to pleasing Jesus at least as much as we are to Him pleasing us.

1- John 3:26

2- Mark 1:5

3- John 3:30

4- Matthew 18:8

5- John 6:56-66

82

Walk by Faith

Three of the weapons that legalists use to make others do what they "should" do are guilt, shame and intimidation.

The other day, a good friend of mine who pastors a church told me that this free will thing is okay but that legalism is much quicker and has better results. I think he is right. When we are encouraging people to witness to their friends, for example, the results would be better if we used the three weapons of legalism, guilt, shame and intimidation. I am not sure we would get the same results if we just announced and encouraged people to witness and then went out and did it ourselves.

We would probably have more people respond to the legalistic way of encouraging good behavior, and after having done it, those same people would feel good about having done it.

The main problem in using the three weapons of legalism is that God never uses them. God respects our free will to the maximum. So, then I have to ask, who do we think we are using methods that God never uses?

Take the case of the rich young ruler in Mark 10. Jesus told him that he had to sell everything he had and give to the poor before coming and following Him.

The young man decided that he was not going to do that. In that moment, if Jesus had given him a good scare (maybe a minor heart attack might have worked) the young man would have seen more clearly, changed his mind, and chosen what was in reality the best for himself.

However, Mark says clearly that Jesus, while loving him, just watched him walk away.

The young man was actually sad when he left.[1] To have made him feel guilty or to have shamed him or intimidated him in some way might have given the desired response immediately.

But there is no evidence in the Word that Jesus even called him back. Jesus totally respected the young man's right to choose.

We do the same thing that the rich young ruler did. When we say the words, "No, Lord" we are not struck by lightening nor does He erase our name from the Book of Life. It seems like nothing happens.

It seems to me that God takes our rejection of His will way too well.

So, seeing it from this perspective, how can we dare impose our criteria or our will on others when Christ never did? Who do we think we are to force anyone to do what we want them to or what we think is right for them?

In the next three chapters, we will look at the three weapons of legalism and explore the danger that lurks in every one of them. Danger for us and danger for other believers.

1-Mark 10:22

84

Guilt

The only motivation that God looks for in us is love. It is the only motivation He has for everything He does. Love does not act unfittingly, is not envious and is not selfish.[1] Love does no ill to its neighbor, therefore love is the fulfilling of the law.[2]

You cannot fulfill the law by your own efforts. I know this from personal experience. Good intentions do not work in obedience to the law. The only way we can do good works with truly pure motives and without being double minded is from a root of agape love.

Agape love is only possible miraculously. This type of love cannot be instilled in another through making them feel guilty. Ever since we were children, we have been made to feel guilty in order to make us do what we should. "There are plenty of children in Africa that would love to have what you have."

Jesus never used this systematic condemnation in His ministry even though He had plenty of opportunities to do so. One example is the woman who was caught in adultery.[3] The Pharisees took her to Jesus expecting Him to react as they had. She was attacked using the three weapons of legalism — condemnation, shame, and fear.

While everyone was waiting for Jesus' decision, He wrote something in the dirt that scared everyone off. Then, finally, He could talk to the woman. He told her that He didn't condemn her and then added, "Go and sin no more". Did she ask for forgiveness for her sin? I don't know that she would have dared.

There is a very distinct difference between the condemnation that we humans use and the conviction for sin that the Lord uses. The difference lies in that the conviction for sin brings hope while condemnation crushes. Condemnation does not leave room for future improvement. Conviction from the Spirit offers possibility to change in that very moment and to have the guilt from our sins never used against us again. I have actually enjoyed feeling the finger of the Lord pointing out something in my life that shouldn't be there, whereas condemnation takes away hope.

Spurgeon told about a time in England when some men were going to blast down a wall. They had lit the fuse and taken cover. One of the men then saw a child walking toward that wall. All the men stood up and began to yell at the child to get out of the way. The child froze and stayed where he was. The mother of the child passed by, saw what was happening, bent down and with her mother's

85

voice softly said, "Son, come to mommy." The child immediately began to run toward his mother and so avoided the blast. It is the kindness of God, not condemnation, that leads us to repentance.

The kindness of God was shown to the woman who was caught in adultery. Both Zaccheus and the sinner who is now writing these words were brought to repentance by hearing "Son, come."

We need to remember that the goal that God has for us is not better behavior but rather, a renewed mind,[4] for us to be changed from glory to glory.[5] We must not use weapons against others that God has renounced to get them to do what is right. If Jesus died to take away our guilt, why do we try to reverse that process?

1- 1 Corinthians 13:5

2- Romans 13:10

3- John 8:1-11

4- Romans 12:2; Ephesians 4:23

5- 2Corinthians 3:18

Shame

To be able to shame someone is a very powerful weapon. It puts the other person in a state of shock. And, if the shame is public, they freeze up.

To do this to a fellow Christian, even with the best of intentions, is not acceptable. We use various methods at different times to shame others, from a dirty look, to publicly singling them out. Often the reason we do this is to change their behavior.

As I said in the previous chapter, we do not have the right to obligate anyone to do anything, ever. God Himself does not obligate us against our will. He respects our free will even while knowing the consequences of our actions. How can we then not respect free will in others?

According to the rules — and God made the rules — every person has the right to make mistakes, to do things wrong and to sin. Many times, with good intentions and with the desire to help others avoid major mistakes, we interfere with their free will. We may get the response we want, but violating other people's free will produces, in the long run, rebellion, resentment and even repulsion on the other person's part for feeling manipulated.

Jesus died to take away our shame. All through His ministry He wanted to dignify sinners, shameful women, lepers and all the outcasts. He did it with me, too. We should never fight against the redemptive work of Jesus, redemptive in every area of our lives.

Rebuke, done right, has it place, but the rules are very clear. Those who are spiritual have to restore someone who has fallen with a humble and meek spirit, recognizing that they, too, can be tempted in the same way.[1] You must not attack the person but rather come alongside them to help them see the damage that they are doing to themselves with their behavior or attitude. The Bible is clear that the wrath of man does not produce the righteousness of God.[2]

These articles about the weapons of legalism are written hoping that you and I can avoid using them against others. I don't ever want to use them again to manipulate anyone for the rest of my life.

Having said that, I want to comment on how we can avoid being shamed by people who want to "help" us with our behavior or attitude.

Paul asks some rhetorical questions. Am I looking to please men or to please

God? He affirms that if he were still a man-pleaser, he would not have been a servant of Christ.[3]

The thing that makes shame so powerful is our very natural desire to please others. Paul knew what God wanted for his life and so could avoid all kinds of attempts to divert him from God's plan, even in the form of a true prophesy telling him that he would be taken prisoner if he went to Jerusalem. He knew what God wanted and that was enough for him.

John talks about people that love the praise of men more than the praise of God.[5] A stunning verse is John 5:44 which asks us how can we believe who receive honor from each other and don't seek the honor that comes only from God?

If we know who we are in God and we know His will for our lives, we can be strong, sure and calm, much less apt to shaming or being shamed.

1- Galatians 6:1

2- James 1:20

3- Galatians 1:10

4- Acts 21:10-14

5- John 12:43

Intimidation

The number one commandment, according to the Word, is to love the Lord our God.[1] But the commandment that is repeated more times than any other is "fear not". God does not want His people to live oppressed by fear.

God has provided everything necessary for us to live free from fear. He told us that we have not received a spirit of slavery that will have us fear again.[2] He affirms that there is no fear in love and that perfect love casts out all fear.[3]

God wants us to have an abundant life and the beating that Jesus took on the day of his crucifixion was a sign of that desire. He took the punishment so we could have peace.[4] He wants us to live securely without the fear of evil.[5]

When we intimidate others in order to impose our will on them, we are going directly against this desire that God has for His people, that we live without fear.

Intimidation can be disguised in various ways, it has many faces. It could be verbal, such as yelling, but also insisting, wearing the other person out, threatening, scorning or ridiculing.

We should never think that it is alright to hurt others in order to produce fear in them and change their wrong behavior. Proverbs tell us that the fear of man brings a snare.[6] We do not help others when we impose our will on them — even when it is for their own good. As a matter of fact, we lay out a snare for them.

One of the greatest fears we have is the fear of rejection. This is the mother of all fears. Ceasing to exist for someone else or for a group of people that we like really hurts, even if it is only momentary.

All of us have experienced rejection in one form or another and we do not want to go through that again. That is why people will often overlook our bad temper, our sarcasm or scorn and will even submit to our manipulations even if they are not convinced that our way of seeing things is the best way. It might be that they don't want to lose our friendship or our approval. God help us not to take advantage of this "weakness" in others. That "weakness" is just a need, a need for love. It shows that those people really value us and our friendship.

We cannot go against God's dream for His people, that they live securely without the fear of evil — even if we are just trying to "help" them to make the right choices.

89

Because of my size, it would be easy for me to intimidate people. I fight against this every day. I use humor to fight against this. God could much more use His "size" to impose His will — which is always the right choice for us to make — but He chooses not to.

My intention in writing these thoughts is to help you and me to resist intimidation and to resist using intimidation as a weapon to "help" people. Let me share with you something that has helped me to resist the threat of intimidation.

Proverbs 19:23 says that the fear of the Lord leads to life and that we can rest satisfied. Strange, isn't it? The fear of the Lord brings life and satisfied rest. Proverbs 14:27 says that the fear of the Lord is a fountain of life. Psalms 27:1 says that God is my light and my salvation and asks a rhetorical question, "whom shall I fear?" It goes on and tells us that the Lord is the strength of our lives and asks again, "of whom shall I be afraid?"

The deeper your relationship with God is, the less susceptible you will be to fear and intimidation. Knowing in whom you have believed gives security and the necessary strength to be able to overcome the manipulations — many times done to "help" you make the right choice — of people that intimidate you.

1- Matthew 22: 36, 37

2- Romans 8:15

3- 1 John 4:18

4- Isaiah 53:5

5- Proverbs 1:33

6- Proverbs 29:25

Only the Young Die Good? (Steve Taylor)

All of us have seen people that started very well in the Christian life. They were very active and sincere. But they did not finish well. You need not worry about this if you are walking in the Spirit.

We are more than conquerors.[1] No weapon formed against us shall prosper. This is the heritage of the servants of the LORD, and their righteousness is of God.[2]

I spoke in another chapter of the fear of being contaminated by people or situations. It is true that in the Old Testament, the unclean contaminated the clean.[3] Now, with the power that Christ gives us, we have authority over evil spirits.[4]

We overcome the enemy by the blood of the Lamb, the word of our testimony and by not loving our lives unto death.[5] Much, much greater is He that is in us than he that is in the world.[6] You are powerful because of He that is within you. Do not be afraid of people or circumstances. Don't focus on them but rather turn your eyes upon Jesus. People or circumstances cannot rob you of what Christ has given you.

Jesus is able to keep us from falling and to present us before the presence of His glory with great joy.[7] He takes care of that.

Sometimes we who have responsibilities to fulfill in the Body of Christ worry about the possibility of our falling and the consequences which follow. We have seen others fall. But we do not have to worry. He takes care of it. "He which has begun a good work in you will perform it until the day of Jesus Christ:"[8]

Of course, I can walk away if I want, but in the same way, I can make it to the end if I want. Not by my striving, but by resting in Him.

He is the Alpha and the Omega.[9] He finishes what He starts. I am clay in His hands. Clay does not decide what shape it is to take. Clay does not mold itself.[10] Clay simply does not resist the potter. That's it.

I have no idea what I am going to turn out like when He is done with me. He has a dream for my life. He has had this dream ever since I was conceived. He loves what I am going to be and is working every day on perfecting me. I submit to Him and let Him do His work in me. He loves me.

91

Instead of worrying about these things — and they are very important things — we need to dedicate ourselves to having that intimate and personal relationship with Christ.

He will guide us in paths of righteousness for His name's sake[11] which is something that we do not know how to do for ourselves. The book of Galatians was written to clear up the confusion that existed about this specific matter. Paul told the Galatians that to start in the Spirit and then end up in our own striving is foolish.[12]

It is easy to fall into the line of thinking that it is up to us and our own efforts to finish well. Our responsibility is to love God with all we are and all we have and to love our neighbor as ourselves.13 Once we dedicate ourselves to these two commandments, we don't have to sweat the other stuff.

Enter into the rest in Him.

_____

1- Romans 8:37

2- Isaiah 54:17

3- Haggai 2:13

4- Mark 16:17

5- Revelation 12:11

6- 1 John 4:4

7- Jude 24

8- Philippians 1:6

9- Revelation 1:8

10- Romans 9:20

11- Psalm 23:3

12- Galatians 3:1

13- Matthew 22:37

14- Matthew 11:28, 29

I'm a Loser (Lennon & McCartney)

I have two friends with whom I feel very close. For some reason, one of them feels that he can only tell me the positive things that are happening in his life and ministry whereas the other feels secure enough in our friendship to tell me about the good, the bad and the ugly that is going on in his life and ministry.

When we see each other, which is not often because all of us are too busy, I feel totally free to talk about my life and ministry to both of them, warts and all. However, the response is different from them. The friend who is comfortable with the idea that I know him as he is, is totally relaxed and comfortable. He is sure of our friendship.

The other friend, however, the one who is not comfortable with me knowing his mistakes or failings, acts insecure and afraid about what I might know, especially if it is going to affect my opinion of him.

The Pharisees were without a doubt, the most respected people in their society. We tend to have an image of them that is nothing like the one their contemporaries had; they considered the Pharisees to be holy, wise and closer to God than the rest of the mere mortals.

But the Pharisees worried about appearances, about their image, about their "good testimony", while Jesus, with all the love He felt for them, wanted them to get rid of their obsession with maintaining a good "front" that only distanced them and isolated them from the rest of the people.[1]

There were other people, outcasts, that did not care about what others thought. They just wanted to get close to Jesus. One was the woman with the issue of blood.[2] According to the law of Moses, she was "unclean".[3] Everyone who touched her, and everything she touched became unclean. On top of her disadvantages, she was a woman, and a sick woman at that. But she did not care. She pushed past everyone who got in her way without worrying about the consequences. This "loser" got to touch Jesus and received healing.

Zacchaeus left his business and ran to climb a tree from where he could see Jesus. He ran the risk that others would mock him, making fun of his small stature. He did not worry about others' respect as much as he wanted to be close to Jesus. He did not care about the dignity that his position afforded. This "loser" took Jesus home with him for lunch and became his friend.[4]

The woman who washed Jesus feet with her tears and dried them with her hair at a dinner in Jesus' honor risked more than any of them. What she did was totally socially unacceptable. She ran the risk of being rebuked by Jesus. (We know how the story ends, but she did not.) According to what Luke tells us, the host of the dinner was a Pharisee. She did not care about others' opinions of her. She wanted to minister to Jesus. This "loser" holds a special place in the Gospels.[5]

So, the Pharisees who wanted to be recognized and admired received a rebuke. Those who did not worry at all about their image received healing and forgiveness.

The approval the world gives is almost always the opposite of the will of God. But if we lose our lives, then we truly win.[6]

I want to be a loser.

1- Matthew 23:13-30

2- Mark 5:25-34

3- Leviticus 15:25-30

4- Luke 19:2-5

5- Luke 7:37-50

6- Matthew 10:39; Mark 16:25; Luke 9:24; 17:33; John 12:25

The Main Thing

I want to share with you a list of areas that I want to grow in that I think are very important both in my personal life and in my ministry.

1) Worship — I want to grow in this ministry to God because He is worthy of praise. I just want my praise to be worthy of Him.

2) Praying in tongues — This is an important part of every one of my days. The first thing I do every morning is to spend time praying in tongues.

3) Prophecy — Paul said that it was the greatest gift.[1] Moses wished that all the people of God prophesied.[2] The Spirit Himself goes a little farther in 1 Corinthians where He says that we may all prophesy. The gift of prophecy is very important.

4) Revelation or insight — As a good friend of mine says, the mysteries of God are not understood, but rather, they are revealed.

5) Knowledge — The prophet said that people are destroyed for a lack of knowledge.[3] Paul prayed every day that they (and we!) would be filled with the knowledge of His will in all wisdom and spiritual understanding.[4]

6) Faith — I want more faith. Without faith it is impossible to please God.[5] Faith moves the hand of God. I want more faith.

7) Generosity — I am an administrator or a steward of another's property. The owner of all that I have in my charge is very generous. I need to be generous, too.

8) Patience in suffering — We are told that if we suffer with Him we will reign with Him. How am I going to face Him if I have never suffered for Him? I don't want to be a coward.

All of us Christians surely want to have all of these things on the list in our lives, our ministry and our church. However there is something so much higher than these very important things in the list above, something that is light years ahead of them.

Let's see what the Scriptures say:

"Though I speak with the tongues of men (worship) and of angels (tongues), and have not charity, I am become as sounding brass, or a tinkling cymbal. And though I have the gift of prophecy, and understand all mysteries (revelation — insight), and all knowledge; and though I have all faith, so that I could remove mountains, and have not charity, I am nothing. And though I bestow all my goods to feed the poor (generosity), and though I give my body to be burned (suffering), and have not charity, it profiteth me nothing."[7]

Loving God above all else is the first and greatest commandment.[8] We can enjoy all of the above in our lives and ministries and even in our churches, but if we don't have the unselfish "agape" love, we don't have anything, we are nothing. Agape love is so much more important than all of these other things together. Without that unselfish passion, they are literally nothing.

Let's keep the main thing the main thing.

1- 1Corinthians 14:1

2- Numbers 11:29

3- Hosea 4:6

4- Colossians 1:9

5- Hebrews 11:6

6- 2 Timothy 2:12

7- 1 Corinthians 13:1-3

8- Matthew 22:37, 38 Mark 12:30 Luke 10:27

Spiritual Authority

At the end of the Sermon on the Mount there is an interesting verse that compares Jesus with some of that day's strongest legalists — the scribes. Matthew says that the people were astonished at Jesus (the Greek word for "astonished" has a connotation of fear, too).

They were so impressed because "he taught them as one having authority, and not as the scribes."[1]

The scribes — along with the legalist that is alive and well in all of us — thought that by preaching the Word, that the authority that the Word has in itself would be transferred to them. But the people listening were not fooled. The people who listened to the scribes on that day had a profound respect for the Word, but they were aware of the lack of authority in ••••••••••••••••••••••

Sadly enough, it seems that those people had become accustomed to listening to sermons preached by teachers that did not have authority. So when the day came that One preached the Word with authority, they were astonished; in fact it kinda scared them a bit.

The legalist in us hopes to obtain authority from merely preaching the Word, or perhaps from a diploma or a position. However, real ministry comes when the authoritative Word of God is shared by a man or woman of God with authority. In these cases, it might even scare the listeners a bit.

So, where does this true personal authority come from? It does not come from positions nor offices. I believe in modern day prophets and apostles, but people are not fooled when someone uses these titles but preaches without authority.

Neither does it come from merely preaching the Word. The Word is powerful. But without the Spirit, it is lethally powerful.[2] It demands total fulfillment of the Law of God[3] (an impossibility to the degree that is demanded by the Word). The Spirit, on the other hand, does not use the Word to make demands, but rather to reveal the heart of God.[4]

Spiritual authority comes from a lifestyle. When He was talking with His disciples about having spiritual authority to cast out a certain brand of demon, Jesus told them that they needed to fast and pray.[5]

But Jesus did not start a fast at that moment, nor do we read that He had a prayer meeting before casting out that demon. Fasting and prayer were a vital part of

97

His lifestyle and as a result He was prepared for that moment. Many of us fast and pray for a specific request. But a lifestyle of fasting and prayer will give us spiritual authority in season and out of season.

The people that listen to us minister — whether they are Christians or pre-Christians — are looking for a river of living water.[6] They are thirsty and want to drink. They will drink any water that is given to them, no matter what the source.

However, if we have flowing out of our innermost being living waters and we give it to them, they will never be thirsty again.[7] And if those living waters are a river, not just a glass or a jug, but a continuous flow, they will want it.

Walk in the Spirit.[8] Get under the tap. Maintain a lifestyle of prayer and fasting. Give them the living water.

1- Matthew 7:28, 29

2- 2 Corinthians 3:6

3- James 2:10, 11

4- Galatians 3:24; 2 Corinthians 3:6   5- Matthew 17:21

6- John 7:38

7- John 4:14; 6:35

8- Galatians 5:16

T'he Leaven of the Pharisees

Those of us who have fallen into legalism probably did it unconsciously, only wanting to please God.

The problem is that when we make this mistake, we have the idea that God is interested in our works. It is hard to believe, when we are in this mindset, that Mary and not Martha was the one who choose the "good part." to think that God must be proud of us, if not grateful for us.

It must have been a huge surprise for the Pharisees to hear Jesus tell people to leave them be, that they were blind guides of the blind, and that the end of their journey would be the ditch.[2]

The Pharisees felt they had the responsibility of raising the standard of holiness for the people of God. They fasted a lot. They went way beyond what the Law required to make sure that they never broke it. (They created 613 rules apart from the commandments to guarantee that the Law would be fulfilled.)

It must have been strange for the disciples and for all of the people who were with Jesus when he said that if their righteousness did not surpass that of the Pharisees they wouldn't enter the Kingdom.[3] The Pharisees were highly respected, even feared, amongst the people. They were considered very superior spiritually because of their great efforts to obey.

It is at the end of His ministry when Jesus' words caused the greatest backlash. In Matthew 23 Jesus rebukes the Pharisees harshly for their inner condition — that which was hidden from the rest of the people by their exterior obedience. Jesus said that the Pharisees did things to be seen by men — doing things for testimony's sake — that they liked receiving honor and respect. They were greedy and their rules did not make any spiritual sense. They were obsessed with the little things.

He also told them that God had wanted to draw them through prophets and wise men, but because the prophets and wise men did not act the way they did and did not sign on with their way of seeing things, the Pharisees had then killed them. He ends His stinging rebuke with the warning that they were a brood of vipers and how did they think they would escape the judgment of hell?[4]

Being a legalist is a serious thing. Hebrews chapters 3 and 4 say that not entering into the rest is disobedience, a lack of faith and hardness of heart. Three times we are told in those two chapters that not ceasing from our own works is to provoke God. Paul was very hard on the legalists in Galatia. He called the Galatians foolish and unwise for following legalists.[5]

He told the Colossians that legalistic teachings appeared to be wise, seemed like good worship and humility. They seemed like a severe treatment of the flesh, but that they have no value against the satisfying of the flesh.[6]

The problem is that we have a mixture in us. We have some left-over legalism in our spirit. Jesus commanded us to guard against the leaven of the Pharisees.[7] He warned that a little leaven will wreck the whole lump.[8]

God help us to recognize this and to have the courage and faith that are necessary to rid our lives of leaven!

1- Luke 10:42

2- Matthew 15:14

3- Matthew 5:20

4- Matthew 23.33

5- Galatians chapter 3

6- Colossians 2:23

7- Matthew 16:6; Mark 8:15; Luke 12:1 81 Corinthians 5:6; Galatians 5:9

More than Conquerors

Two of the sweetest little girls in the world came up to me in a church one day. They were crying. When I asked them what was wrong, they told me that some young people had told them that the Mickey Mouse t-shirt one of them was wearing was of the devil.

Man, was I ticked off! Not only for the young people's lack of wisdom (after all they are young) but more than anything, for the message they were sending to these little impressionable girls. We do not have to be careful with Disney, Disney needs to be worried about us.

In the Old Testament, corruption was powerful. If a clean thing touched an unclean thing, the holy became abominable and contaminating.[1] If you touched a leper, a dead body or an animal that was not on the "acceptable" list, you were defiled and had to follow certain rites to become acceptable to God and society again.

However, everything changes in the New Testament. The victory that cost Jesus so much is absolute. Now, if I touch a leper, he just might be healed.[2] There even exists the possibility that a dead man might rise from the dead if I touch him, rather than his dead body contaminating mine.[2]

So, we don't have to fear external contamination.[3] The power that is in us is so superior that any external contaminating elements should fear us.

We should go to the company Christmas party, kick in the door and declare, "The light has arrived."

But, as long as we see ourselves as weak, well, we are. If we are afraid of being contaminated, we will worry and protect ourselves from that contamination more than we will work at being salt and light[4], at being friends of sinners[5] or being in the world but not of the world. We need to be casting out demons, healing the sick and preaching the kingdom of God.[6]

God does reign. Greater is He that is in us than he that is in the world.[7] We are more than conquerors through Him who loves us.[8]

He who did not even spare His own Son but put Him through what He went through for us, won't He give us everything else along with it?[9] Who can be against us?[10] (I want to tell you a secret. These are rhetorical questions.)

101

I am not a triumphalist. But when I believe something that contradicts what the Bible says, I am not being a realist, I am believing a lie. And if I live as if this lie were true, I am missing out on everything that Jesus bought for me at a very high price. This false modesty that we Christians can be guilty of, is in reality a lack of faith.

If I have my eyes on my heavenly home, if I consider myself a pilgrim and stranger on this earth, all that is attractive here fades. The gates of hell do not attack me●Þam the one who attacks the gates of hell and they cannot resist.[11]

Let us take our rightful place. We are children of the Most High and everything has been provided for my personal victory and my ministry in the world.

1- Haggai 2:13

2- Matthew 10:8

3- Mark 7:19; Matthew 15:11-20

4- Matthew 5:14

5- Matthew 11:19; Luke 7:34; Luke 15:2

6- Matthew 10:8

7- 1John 4:4

8- Romans 8:37

9- Romans 8:32

10- Romans 8:31

11- Matthew 16:18

Led by the Spirit

To be led by the Spirit is much more than just finding the will of God in times of making big decisions or when the circumstances of our lives are not what we want them to be. Being led by the Spirit is a lifestyle.

Paul wrote that those that are led by the Spirit of God are the children of God.[1] What a privilege it is to feel the nudges of the Spirit, to "see" things in His Word (not just understand, but to "see them"). What a joy to experience how the Spirit reveals things to us as if a light were turned on whereas before there was only darkness when we studied the Bible or listened to a sermon.

And what He reveals to us in that moment may or may not have to do with the thing we were studying or the sermon we were listening to. I am sure this has happened to you. But the great thing is that you can live daily in this intimate, personal relationship with God. Often, however, other things take the place of the Spirit's guidance I tell you that from my own experience.

In my case, one thing that took the Spirit's place and became my guide was reason, or we might say, logic. Many other Christians who had been saved longer than me encouraged me in this error saying things like "God gave us a brain for a reason" or "God does not want us to park our thought process or our mind when we give our lives to Him", etc. But the Spirit was being quenched and grieved in my life.

God opened up scriptures to me like "Trust in the Lord with all thine heart and lean not unto thine own understanding. In all thy ways acknowledge Him and He shall direct thy paths."[2] And that is what I want! I want Him to direct my paths but I had no idea of how to obtain that.

It is just like God says when He tells us that His thoughts are not our thoughts nor are His ways our ways.[3] So my reasoning is NOT His. His thoughts are so much higher, like the heavens are above the earth. So what I need, beyond my learning and my experience, is that my mind be renewed,[4] that the Lord will give me understanding in all things.

I was also encouraged to allow circumstances to guide me. But this didn't last long as I saw clearly in my life and in the Bible that many, many times circumstances were totally opposite to what God wanted and that the Lord used them to try me or to give Himself the opportunity to do a miracle. In 1 Samuel 13, King Saul let himself be led by circumstances and lost his kingdom.

103

Another mistake that I made was to put the guidance of His Word in the place of the guidance of the Spirit.

The Word of God is totally important for every believer, but the Spirit of God is more important still. The Spirit inspired the Scriptures. They are His. I believe that the Bible is the Word of God, infallible, totally inspired and as 1 Timothy 3:16 says "profitable for teaching." But it is a tool that the Spirit uses to lead us into all truth. The Word of God is subservient to God.

The Scriptures do not say "I leave you my book which will lead you into all truth." Nor do they say "They that are led by the Bible, they are the children of God." He did not say "You need not that any man teach you as the New Testament itself teaches you all things."

I know the Bible, from Genesis to maps. I have taught it many years in the Bible school here in Spain — especially the Old Testament. I read the Bible every single day and I feed from it. But Paul himself said, "Who also hath made us able ministers of the new testament; not of the letter, but of the spirit: for the letter killeth, but the spirit giveth life."[6]

The Spirit uses the Word to talk to me. How many times have I been reading the Bible and realized that it was dry or incomprehensible to me that day. But when the Spirit gets ahold of it, it goes right down to my joints and marrow and discerns the thoughts and intents of my heart.[7]

So, I am fighting to keep the main thing the main thing. I want the first thing to be first. I want my relationship to be with the Lord.

I want everything to point me back to Him who loved me and gave Himself for me.[8]

1- Romans 8:14

2- Proverbs 3:5,6

3- Isaiah 55:8

4- Ephesians 4:23

5- 2Timothy 2:7

6- 2 Corinthians 3:6

7- Hebrews 4:12

8- Galatians 2:20

The Fruit of the Spirit

One of the greatest gifts that God has given us is the fruit of the Spirit. Yes, it is a gift. Or do you think we have done something to deserve it? The fruit grows in us because we have been grafted into Him.

The legalist who resides in us fervently desires the fruit of the Spirit. However, he cannot enjoy it because of his view of Christianity. The fruit of the Spirit is not earned; it is the result of a loving relationship.

Let's take a look at the first three fruits of the Spirit mentioned in the list in Galatians 5.

Love (Agape) This is a totally selfless love. It is very difficult for the legalist in us to believe that anyone loves him unselfishly. He sees Christianity as based on performance and output and so believes that he receives only the love he deserves. When he is submitted and obedient, God loves him more. When he is rebellious or distracted, the love is proportionally less.

So because he believes that this is how God loves, it is understandable that he feels that he should love others in the same way. **The legalist sees unconditional love as something dangerous.**

Sadly, the legalist residing in all of us tries to pressure God Himself by using the same method. If God does not fulfill our expectations of Him, we punish Him by not going to church, not praying any more, by taking things into our own hands and resolving things in our own way instead of waiting on Him. In that way we show God that His behavior has not been acceptable. I am not sure if Jesus laughs or cries when He sees this childish behavior in us.

The second fruit on the list is **Joy.** Why are those that emphasize God's righteousness so cranky? The answer is because they believe that they have to be cranky. They can only give their approval when the behavior is acceptable and as "acceptable behavior" is so scarce these days, disapproval is the only alternative that the legalist has.

But joy is a very important part of the Christian life. Jesus said, "...no one will take your joy away from you."[1] We have joy in tribulation[2] and joy in affliction.[3]. "For the kingdom of God is not meat and drink; but righteousness, and peace, and joy in the Holy Ghost."[4] Can a life without joy be called a truly "Christian life"?

105

But the legalist in me despises joy. Religion is a very serious thing, the legalist affirms.

The third fruit is **Peace**. Hopefully, we all understand that God wants us to enjoy peace — always. Peace in the morning, peace in the evening, in every waking moment, peace. (He is a good Father) "The chastisement of our peace was upon Him."[5] (In other words, He took the beating so we could have peace.) Is there any epistle in the New Testament that does not start with the stated desire that the readers enjoy peace?

This has nothing to do with the circumstances of our lives.[6] It has everything to do with our relationship with God. He is our peace.[7] A lack of peace isn't a sign of being in touch with the reality of our times nor does it mean that I am taking serious things seriously. It shows a lack of prayer and faith.[8] "…to be spiritually minded is life and peace."[9] We should not brag about how stressed out we are nor how worried we are. It should worry you if you are worried. Jesus wants you to have peace.[10]

1- John 16:22

2- James 1:2

3- 2 Corinthians 12:10

4- Romans 14:17

5- Isaiah 53:5

6- Phillipians 4:7

7- Ephesians 2:14

8- Phillipians 4:6, 7

9- Romans 8:6

10- John 16:33

Dressing up to Go Out

One of the most moving things that Jesus said to us is in chapter 15 of the Gospel of John. Here Jesus said that we did not choose Him, but he chose us.[1]

We, as born-again Christians, emphasize the personal decision that we make when we give our lives to the Lord. The old saying that "God doesn't have grandkids" is true; He only has kids. Everyone has to respond to His call individually.

However, we should not forget the importance that the Bible places on God's role in our salvation. It clearly says that we love Him because He first loved us.[2] Jesus said that we cannot go to Him unless the Father draws us.[3]

This is a liberating truth. He wanted us! That is why He paid the stipulated price to redeem us. He sought us out and drew us to Himself.

When we finally responded to His call, He took us in with joy. He did all this because He loves us.

We know that we are the children of a loving God, but do we know what He expects from us? He is not expecting perfection, but rather, holiness.

The perfectionist can run into serious difficulties in the Christian life. He can get impatient, harsh, and demanding when God Himself is not impatient, harsh or demanding.

Holiness is not obtained but rather imparted. Paul encourages us to put off the old man who is corrupted by lusts and deceit. He tells us to be renewed in the spirit of our mind and to put on our new selves in whom the likeness of God is created in righteousness and true holiness.[4]

We don't try to reform the old man but rather to get rid of him, put him off.

In the Old Testament, the priests had to clothe themselves according to very exacting stipulated rules given by God. In the New Testament, we, the royal priesthood have to, also.

After we put off the old man, we have to put on the Lord Jesus Christ,[5] put on love,[6] and put on our new self, created in the likeness of God.[7]

I can't tell you how to put on Christ, the new man, or how to put on love. These

107

are things that are reserved exclusively for your heavenly Father and I am just your brother. I don't know how to explain it. You need to ask Him directly. Wait on Him and He will answer.

We do not strive to be perfect nor to be holy. We put on Christ, put on the new man, put on love, and then we walk with our head held a little higher.

Someone once said that no one is perfect, until you fall in love with that one. Then they are perfect for you.

God is in love with you.

1- John 15:16;

2- 1 John 4:19

3- John 6:44

4- Ephesians 4:22-24

5- Romans 13:14

6- Colossians 3:14

7- Ephesians 4:24